RESCUED FROM THE DRAGON

True Accounts from China

Alice Hayes Taylor

marshalls

Marshalls Paperbacks
Marshall Morgan & Scott
3 Beggarwood Lane, Basingstoke, Hants, RG23 7LP, UK

Copyright © 1982 Light and Life Press
First published by Light and Life Press in the United States
First published in the United Kingdom by
Marshall Morgan & Scott 1984

ISBN 0 551 01126 2

Printed in Great Britain by Anchor Brendon Ltd, Tiptree,
Colchester.

PREFACE

As I have traveled from place to place participating either in evangelistic meetings or in missionary conventions and have recounted outstanding conversions that we witnessed in China, friends have frequently come at the close of the service and suggested that these experiences be written in a book so that many more people may enjoy them. Consequently *Rescued from the Dragon* has been produced.

In Revelation 20:2 we read, "He seized the dragon, that ancient serpent, who is the devil, or Satan, and bound him" (Revelation 20:2 NIV). In China people make elaborate paintings of the dragon, carve intricate wooden figures of him, embroider him on their clothing, wear gold dragon ornaments, build temples in his honor, and worship him. Most of these worshipers are held under the power of Satan until the Mighty Conqueror binds him and sets them free. Hence the title of this book. Sometimes the word dragon means China, but that is not the usage here.

Since human need as well as human failure is practically the same in every civilization and culture, I have written these accounts with the hope that they will be a personal blessing to those who read them and will also inspire each one to take advantage of contacts he has with others to help them find relief from the power of Satan that binds them.

I regret that it has not been possible for me to obtain consent to publish these life stories from those whose experiences are narrated in this book. Many have already gone to be with their Maker; with others still living in China communication is difficult. For obvious reasons I have used fictitious names of persons and have not identified the exact location of incidents.

During the Cultural Revolution in China many church buildings were destroyed. Others were closed or used by the authorities for various purposes. In spite of this, the work of God continues to go forward. Some churches are now reopening. Many more believers are worshiping in homes. Competent observers estimate that the number of Christians has increased from one million to ten, twelve, or even fifty million in the past thirty years. Christ's promise to Peter is still the same today, "I will build my church and the gates of hell will not overcome it" (Matthew 16:18 NIV). Scripture references are from the New International Version unless otherwise indicated.

Rescued from the Dragon goes forth with prayer that readers will rejoice in our Lord's transforming power, and remember Christians in China today, praying that God will give them courage and fortitude to be faithful to Him even in the most extreme persecution, and that fearful ones will not draw back from trusting in the One who never fails.

Alice Hayes Taylor

TABLE OF CONTENTS

Preface

Chapter One

BAMBOO PRINCESS

FORGIVEN MUCH, SHE LOVED MUCH

With aching dread the little girl sat sobbing on the front step of her home. Her mother had been very sick. Now she lay still! *Why doesn't she answer and take me into her arms?* the little girl wondered.

In the corner of the courtyard her older brother sat forlorn with fearful forebodings. *What will now become of Bamboo Princess and me?*

A crowd was already gathering outside the front gate of their farm home in South China. Word had spread quickly through the community that their father and mother had died within a few hours of each other of that dread disease, cholera. Neighbors dared not venture inside the house to care for the burial of the dead. The children had, of course, been exposed. They too could contract the horrible disease momentarily. Surely their maternal uncle would come and take the children to his home.

"Who will go for their mother's brother?" shouted one of the neighbors to the whispering crowd.

"I will," replied another. Jumping on his bicycle he pedaled quickly away, balancing himself skillfully on the narrow footpaths that separated the recently planted rice paddies.

The crowd thinned. The people followed the clever cyclist with their eyes. Help would soon arrive and a plan would be made for the newly orphaned children.

In the afternoon people gathered again when Mr. Lee, the children's uncle, arrived. He invited some bystanders to help him lay the bodies into the cheap board coffins he had bought. At the same time he ordered both children to take sticks of lighted incense in their hands and kneel before the coffins. Even had she thought, Bamboo Princess could not have realized that this would be the final reverential act of respect she and her brother would pay their parents.

A few neighbors helped to carry the coffins out to the field and buried them in a shallow grave, mounding a pile of earth over them. The half-burned smoking joss sticks were planted in the loose dirt. Mr. Lee did not take time to pile up the usual high mound of earth over the coffins. There would never be anyone to keep up the graves, or to come to worship the deceased, so why should he worry about a large mound of earth as a memorial to his sister and her husband? Callously his thoughts turned to how he would have to assume responsibility for the children, and what a burden that would add to his family. The boy was only six and Bamboo Princess four. They were far too young to help much with his farm work. Why did his sister and her husband have to die at the same time and leave two more mouths for him to feed?

After caring for a few of his sister's affairs, Mr. Lee sullenly picked up his niece in one arm and let her brother sit on the back carrier of his bicycle as he started for home with the two unwanted charges. His wife spoke no word of kindly welcome to the frightened orphans when he reached home.

"Have we not enough children of our own? Why must we feed and clothe two more?" she grumbled heartlessly.

The woman coldly sized up the children as they stood wide-eyed at the door. The boy would sweep the courtyard and take care of his little sister while she and her husband and children went out to work in their paddy fields, she thought. Gradually they would let the lad help with transplanting rice and later hilling up by hand each individual plant after it had taken root. Perhaps they would be able to make something out of the boy. But what would they do with Bamboo Princess?

To poor peasant people, a girl was a liability. They would have to feed and clothe her until she was about sixteen when they could get her married into some home. That would involve money, a lot of money. There had to be some way to relieve them of this burden. A small bowl of food was grudgingly measured for her at each meal, hardly enough to sustain life. They soon taught her to sweep the house and the courtyard and to wash clothes at the nearby stream.

Nine lonely years dragged by. Bamboo Princess didn't miss the rollicking joys of childhood. She never knew them! As the girl began to mature, her uncle and aunt could not but notice how beautiful she was.

"And beauty sells," said Mrs. Lee to her husband one day. "I can make her some pretty clothes, rub perfumed oil into her hair, maybe even plait a pretty artificial flower into her braid. . . ."

"Isn't she charming?" exclaimed her aunt some days later when she had completed the make-up. "You should be able to get several hundred dollars for her. Take her into the city at once. See which brothel offers the most. We need the cash."

Bamboo Princess could hardly believe her ears. The only relative she had! He had even given her his surname when her mother had died! Was it possible that now he was carrying her away to sell as a prostitute? The new clothes, the perfume, the flower in her hair — suddenly she understood it all. She wanted

15

desperately to jump down from the bicycle and run away. But where could she go? Unaware of the evil plot, her brother was hard at work in the fields. She had not another friend in the world. Only an orphan girl! She would have to submit to her uncle's wishes.

He took her to several houses of ill repute and finally accepted the best offer. Bamboo Princess saw him smiling at the good deal he had made for himself as he counted the roll of money. With not so much as a word he was back on his bicycle and gone. Bamboo Princess cried herself to sleep that first night and many nights thereafter. In anguish she often would call out, "Mother! Mother! Why did you die and leave me?"

Still too young to ply the trade for which she had been sold, she could watch the older girls and learn the business while she swept floors, scoured wash basins, and cleaned spittoons during the day. As she observed the other prostitutes, her whole being rebelled against such a life. More than once she wished she were dead. That nagging thought kept coming with increasing frequency. How could she take her own life? Her owner had spent much money to buy her and to feed her. She had no money with which to buy poison, nor did she know what to buy. Night after night she cried herself to sleep, "Mother! Mother! What can I do?"

To add to her insecurity, approaching armies made it necessary for her owner to move his whole business to Nanking to get away from the war and its bombings. Soon she was old enough to take up the business for which he had bought her. She ached with fear, yet what alternative was there but to conform to his wishes. Loathsome night followed loathsome night.

Bamboo Princess knew she would rather die than continue such a life. One day when she went out for a walk along the street, she dropped into a medicine shop and bought a package of poison. Her mind was now made up. She would slip away at the earliest opportunity, go to the Yangtse River, take a dose of poison and then jump in. If the poison did not kill her, the river would; and her miserable existence would be over.

Bamboo Princess had never heard of God. She had only seen people worshiping idols in the temple near her aunt's home. Not once had she ever heard of the true God, or His love, or of the power of prayer.

A few nights later her opportunity seemed to come. Tucking the packet of poison into her pocket, she walked slowly northward out of the city until she stood at the river bank. Just as she was about to take the poison and plunge into the river, she seemed to hear a clear voice calling, "Bamboo Princess, Bamboo Princess, go back!"

Quickly slipping the poison back into her pocket, she looked up to see who was calling her. But she could see no one. Astonished at the words she had heard, she pondered, *Go back? Go back to what? I cannot endure this kind of life any longer. I would rather die now.*

Though she could see no one, the voice was unmistakable. Perhaps life did hold something better for her after all. There in the darkness she resolved to return to her owner and see what it might be. Desolate days followed the horror of each night as rumors of the advancing Japanese armies filled her heart with an aching fear.

One night a well-dressed businessman stepped into the front teahouse. Later he came to her room. Mr. Chang was older and seemed to be more merciful than many of the others. As Bamboo Princess sat talking to him, she suddenly burst into tears. "I was not born to lead this kind of life," she cried. "My whole person rebels against it. If this is all that remains for me in life, I prefer to die now. Can't you buy me

17

out of this place so that I can make a respectable living?"

Chang's heart was touched by her earnest entreaties. Yet he was a profligate man. As a teenager in northern China, he had become so debauched and wicked that his own father had driven him from home. "You are such a disgrace to our family," he said, "I never want to see your face again. Go to Peking. Lose yourself among the crowds where you are not known. Write if you need money, but never come back home again."

Off he had gone with great joy, realizing that no longer would there be a restraining hand on his shoulder when he wanted to have a fling. His days were filled with gambling, drinking, and licentiousness. He had married four times. Two of his wives died of ill treatment at his hand, and one left him. The fourth was an educated woman who gave birth to five gifted children. She heard of Christ when she attended church several times. Occasionally she had sent the children to Sunday school, but her husband cared nothing for religious matters.

Now, because of the war, he had left home and was carrying on some business in other parts of China. His wife and three children remained in Peking while two of the older ones were away from home attending a wartime college.

As Chang listened to Bamboo Princess tell her story, his heart was touched. He persuaded the owner of the establishment to reserve Bamboo Princess for him alone until he could get together the money necessary to redeem her. She was beautiful and he also recognized that this was a young woman of character, very much worth saving. He did not intend to keep her as his own concubine, but rather to have her marry some friend who had no wife. However, he had no place to take her except to his own room, nor could he think of any friend who was suitable for her. So they began living together as man and wife.

Bamboo Princess soon learned that Chang had his own wife and family. She was not happy with this type of relationship, yet in his presence could say nothing against it because it would make her seem ungrateful for all the money he had spent to redeem her. He could not understand why she continued to be unhappy. He bought her jewelry and pretty clothes and often took her to the theater at night. Though he bought her the most expensive foods, she had no appetite. Nothing brought happiness. She became thinner and thinner. Chang was afraid Bamboo Princess would die.

As the war raged on, they moved farther north and west, into the country and away from the bombings. On one occasion they fled from a town just a few hours before the building in which they had been living was razed to the ground by enemy bombs. Chang began to wonder why God had spared their lives.

In the small town to which they had now moved, the Christian church was having special evangelistic services. Chang remembered that the Christians he had known were happy, and so he decided to send Bamboo Princess to the services, hoping that she would find happiness there. One of the neighbor women escorted her to church.

Bamboo Princess was deeply impressed by the story of Christ who loved sinners and gave His life for them on the cross. She listened carefully during the services for several days. Many told of peace and joy in their hearts after they found the Lord.

Then one day she decided to see whether Christ would take her. Could His salvation also include a concubine who hated her way of life? She wore her prettiest clothing that Sunday morning and rubbed perfumed oil on her hair to make herself as attractive to Christ as possible. Would He accept her, or would He turn her away? Fully intending to go forward with other seekers at the close of the evangelistic message, she was determined to find the same peace of heart that others were telling about.

That morning the evangelist spoke of the love of God for sinners, but in the course of his message he surprisingly said, "There is no forgiveness for a concubine. Not only is she herself on the way to hell, but she is also dragging the man with whom she is living to hell."

Bamboo Princess heard no more. It seemed that mentally she just blanked out. Cold chills went up and down her spine, as inconspicuously she left the church. At home she wept with bitter disappointment. *So I am already damned,* she thought. Bamboo Princess refused to attend any more services. What was the use? There was neither forgiveness nor joy for a concubine. Only the fires of hell awaited her.

Chang was beside himself trying to find new comfort for her. Since the Japanese armies were again threatening, he and Bamboo Princess packed up their things and moved farther west, where he hoped again to establish his industrial enterprise.

The flow of refugees from the east had created a critical housing crisis. Providentially, however, they found a house with a courtyard not far from the railroad station, and in a short time Chang had his industry going again.

One day he met Lu-chia, a man who had built a hotel near the railroad station, who told him that he and his wife, Ruth, had recently become Christians. Since the two families lived near each other, the women often met when they went shopping for vegetables.

Bamboo Princess was surprised to learn that

Lu-chia's wife had also lived the life of a concubine, having done it by choice so that she could marry a wealthy man. Ruth had even driven the first wife away from the home and had taken the two children as her own. Yet Ruth had been born again and was happy in the joy of the Lord. She was earnest in prayer and Bible reading every day. *If God could save her, why could He not save me?* Bamboo Princess thought.

Though Ruth invited her to go with her to the church services, Bamboo Princess declined repeatedly because she did not want to revive her hopes of salvation only to have them dashed again.

Ruth and her husband had a home about a hundred miles away from the hotel where they often went to live. In fact, they spent most of their time at this home because of repeated bombings in the provincial capital. Bamboo Princess really missed her frequent visits with Ruth. As the days went by, she thought over the question that now almost haunted her: *Why can Ruth receive forgiveness from the Lord when I cannot?* She had no appetite for food. Meal after meal she turned away from the most savory dishes after barely sampling them. Once again she began to lose weight and Chang became alarmed.

One morning Bamboo Princess asked him if she might take a trip to see Ruth.

"Go anywhere you like if it will only make you happy," he replied.

She quickly packed an overnight bag and hurried off to the railroad station to catch the morning train.

All day long as the train moved at what seemed a snail's pace, she kept thinking, *Can I ask Ruth how to become a Christian? Have I the courage to tell her my whole story? Is there any hope that God can give me the joy that Ruth has?*

Only a month before this, God had directed James and me to that very city and to that very home. We had been guided to go to China's northwest to open a new work and to start a Bible school for the training of young people for the Christian ministry. We had gone out very much as Abraham did, not knowing where we were going, but with the firm confidence that God would guide us step by step to the very place where He wanted us to be.

It was Lu-chia and Ruth who took us into their home. They kindly vacated their own living room for our use, while they moved into a room half the size. We had daily Bible study with them and prayed earnestly and repeatedly that the Lord would guide as to where He would have us open the Bible school. The first few weeks, heavy rains prevented our moving about, but this gave us more time to wait on the Lord for His guidance.

One night after sitting in the courtyard talking over spiritual matters with Lu-chia and Ruth, we retired to our room. A gentle knock on the front gate aroused us. We could hear our host and someone else talking with subdued voices. Since the visitor had not come for us, we soon dropped off to sleep again.

Early the next morning Ruth came into our room and told us Bamboo Princess's story and asked whether God could save such a person, and whether there was any hope of forgiveness for her? Ruth said, "You know she has come over a hundred miles to ask this question."

"Of course, God can forgive her," we replied. "She is more sinned against than sinning. Is it not God who has put this hunger for himself in her heart? Please bring her in."

Reassured, though timid, the graceful Bamboo Princess entered and sat down. After explaining simply to her the way to peace with God, we knelt together in prayer. After she had prayed only a short time, her faith finally found that resting place, the joy of the

Lord came to her heart, and a beautiful smile spread over her face. She arose and quietly told us that Christ had come into her heart.

Bamboo Princess remained with us for several days all the while gaining a better understanding of the Scriptures and of the Christian life. One problem still troubled her — how could she leave Chang without making him feel she was ungrateful? We urged her not to act hastily but to wait patiently in prayer until God worked a complete release for both of them.

By this time word had reached Chang's wife, Meilan, in Peking that her husband had taken to himself an attractive young concubine with whom he was living in luxury in the northwest. Her jealousy and spiteful anger knew no bounds. Immediately, she sent a letter to the two older children who were away in college instructing them to meet her at their father's home, as she was setting out for there with the three young children and wanted the entire family to be together.

She bought a revolver determining that after she had everyone under one roof, right before Chang's eyes she would shoot all of the children, Bamboo Princess, her husband, and finally herself. She would show him that she would never allow him to continue such an outrage against her and the family. Had she not cared for his children all this long time he had been away from home, taking full responsibility for their support? She would show him! The nearer she got to him, the fiercer her anger became.

With her three children Meilan escaped enemy-occupied territory, crossed no man's land, and finally reached the Chinese side. When she arrived at Chang's home, she was met at the front gate by a sweet and composed Bamboo Princess. Meilan was taken aback. Some strange restraining power seemed to be at work in her. She decided to just watch

Bamboo Princess for a few days. She noticed that she read her Bible and prayed every day and that there was a joy and serenity about her that she herself did not possess.

After giving the matter saner thought Meilan decided not to destroy the whole family after all. Instead she made a plan for each one: the two college students would return to school; Chang would set up a home with Bamboo Princess and the youngest child at the factory one hundred miles away; while she herself would occupy the city residence and keep the two teenagers with her.

Bamboo Princess was not at all happy with the plan, as it would prevent her from getting a complete release from Chang. But she went where she was sent and began living in the factory home just three miles from where we were having services. She attended regularly.

One weekend when Meilan came to visit Chang in their factory home, Bamboo Princess invited her to attend the service which was held in our room. That morning the Holy Spirit spoke to Meilan's heart, and in tears she knelt and confessed her sins and found forgiveness and reconciliation. She went back to her city home to live for the Lord. Now Bamboo Princess prayed more hopefully than ever for the salvation of Chang. She was convinced that if he became a Christian he would be willing to release her.

Shortly after the conversion of Meilan, Bamboo Princess invited us to her home to have dinner with Chang and his little girl. When the meal was ready Chang came over from his factory office. He was the picture of dissipation, yet so successful in every business venture he turned to. How proud and arrogant he looked!

After we were seated at the table, I quietly turned the conversation to spiritual concerns and his need of

God. Normally Chang would have cursed anyone who intimated that he was in any way lacking in morality. But somehow this time he listened. We shared with him the love of God for sinners and urged him to let Christ set him free from his sinful habits. He was so interested in what we were saying that he almost forgot to eat. Unfortunately, other duties necessitated our return home after the dinner. That night we prayed earnestly for Chang and we knew that Bamboo Princess was praying, too.

To our surprise Chang came to our home the next day to ask questions he had about the gospel, but business matters took him away after an hour's talk. The following Sunday he came into the city with Bamboo Princess and went to dinner with a friend prior to attending the afternoon service in our room.

Just as he was setting out from his friend's home for the meeting, a dust storm came up. This was most unusual for the northwest area. Pink, ominous clouds filled the sky, while dust and leaves swirled through the air. The regular attendants dared not venture out to the service that day for fear of a tornado. But Chang blew into Lu-chia's courtyard fuming that he had ruined his Palm Beach suit and Panama hat in the terrible dust storm. Ruth was equal to the situation. Had she not calmed an angry husband more than once? Taking Chang's suit coat and hat, she brushed them off and polished his gold-headed cane. She gave him a basin of warm water and soap to wash his face and hands. In a short time the tempest in his heart quieted, and he sat down for the service.

Only Chang, Bamboo Princess, and another Christian woman named Julia had ventured out in the storm to attend the service that afternoon. Clearly God had chosen a select group who could help Chang pray. He listened attentively again as a simple gospel message was directed to him and his need. When we asked whether he would like to become a Christian Chang responded immediately by kneeling on a newspaper which Ruth spread on the brick floor of our room. He began to confess his sins to God.

Some of us could hardly imagine that human beings could commit some of the sins that Chang confessed. After a time he just stood up. That bulldog look on his bleared face was gone. It seemed that it had now been replaced by a light from heaven. He had found peace with God. He was a new man in Christ Jesus.

Chang immediately disposed of all sorts of equipment that had enslaved him so long: cigarettes, cigars, pipes, and an opium pipe. He began telling all of his friends what God had done for him. People could hardly believe their eyes and ears. The man who had been known all over that area for his licentious living now sat with a Bible in hand, tears coursing down his cheeks as he told of the transformation that God had made in his heart and life. No one could doubt its genuineness because his life backed up his testimony.

Bamboo Princess was so happy that Chang had found the Lord; however, his conversion did not solve her problems immediately. She began to feel that God was leading her to take training in the Northwest Bible Institute and prepare herself for the Lord's work. But how could she become free from Chang? He had come to love and admire her for her genuine character. And if free, where would her support come from?

Bamboo Princess told me of her struggle and we often prayed together. One day while Chang was talking with us about baptism we frankly shared with him that his relationship with Bamboo Princess was not honoring to God. We also mentioned that since she felt called to the Lord's work, he should allow her to study at the Bible school.

Chang asked whether all this was our idea or was it Bamboo Princess's? We assured him that it was entirely hers. I told him of the times she had shared her struggle with me, fearing that he would feel she was ungrateful, yet sensing God's clear call to service.

He replied, "She will die eating the coarse unappetizing food that the Bible school students eat. If she eats so little of the delicacies I provide for her, what will she do there? I cannot bear to see her suffer."

"If God is guiding in this, He will help her enjoy the simple, coarse food," was our reply. "Let her come to the school and try it and see how she gets along."

Chang agreed, and a very happy Bamboo Princess set out for the Bible school. Chang paid all her expenses. Unbelievable as it must have seemed to him, from the beginning Bamboo Princess relished the food. She began to gain weight, and a healthy color came into her cheeks. She applied herself to Bible study; and when students went out in the open air to evangelize, she was one of the most forceful speakers as she testified to the transforming power of Christ. She was becoming an effective soul winner.

A baptism service was planned for the new converts at the Chinese New Year in early February. Chang wanted to be baptized. Some had reservations, feeling that his matrimonial problems should first be resolved. He fully agreed. Having seen how Bamboo Princess was improving in health and how she cared about souls, he sat down and wrote out a check for a large sum of money which he deposited in the bank to her name. From the interest received on the money she would be able to pay all her living expenses for many years to come. Chang also drew up legal papers releasing Bamboo Princess from any further obligation or relationship to him.

Though it was still winter, the Christians prayed that the sun would come out and warm things up a bit for the people who were to go down into the cold water of the river for baptism. God answered prayer and during the few sunny hours of the Chinese New Year day, Chang, Meilan, Bamboo Princess, and others received baptism in the river. It was a precious and memorable occasion. Chang and Bamboo Princess were both free in two senses of the word.

Chang and Meilan opened their home near the railroad station in the provincial capital for services and many of his friends and employees found the Lord. There in his living room day after day services were conducted afternoon and evening until a flourishing church was organized.

After graduation from the Northwest Bible Institute, Bamboo Princess joined the Back-to-Jerusalem Band. This Chinese missionary organization had a vision of carrying the gospel to Muslim communities on the western borders of China and on, all the way back to Jerusalem. Bamboo Princess gave the full measure of her life for Christ in this service.

Chapter Two

LU-CHIA

THE YOUNG MARSHALL'S OFFICER

"You mean that you want to be a soldier like your father!" shouted Mrs. Sung to her eldest son, "Can't you find a more honorable occupation than that?"

"No, Mother," Lu-chia replied, "In the past people despised a soldier. But now, since the days of the Republic, the moral and educational standards and qualifications have been raised. People everywhere respect men in military service. Moreover, young people have an obligation to help unite the country and make China one of the great world powers. Yes, I want to be a soldier. I am enlisting today."

Lu-chia joined the army under Chang Hsueh-liang, the Young Marshall from Manchuria who had high hopes for the future of this country. By intensive training and proven dependability, he became a part of the private escort of the Young Marshall, traveling everywhere with him.

In the meantime, his parents, carrying out the custom of the times, chose for him a wife. She was illiterate with small bound feet. To this couple a daughter and a son were born. Since his wife had never been educated, she remained in Lu-chia's mother's home and cared for the children and for her husband whenever he came home.

As Lu-chia was promoted to higher rank and his salary increased, he developed harmful habits and wicked ways, often accompanying the other officers to visit the bars and the brothels. At one of these places he met an attractive young woman named Ruth, who seemed to have a special affinity for him. Night after night he visited her; and the more he saw her, the better he liked her.

Like Lu-chia, Ruth had been a strong-willed, rebellious teenager. When she was fifteen, her mother had called her to her side one day and said, "Ruth, it is already past time for us to engage you to a husband. You have always repulsed us every time we have approached the subject with you."

"Yes," interrupted Ruth, "and I still don't want you to make plans for me. I want to choose my own husband. Lots of girls are making their own choices today."

"But Ruth," her mother protested, "the Wang family who lives on the big farm is interested in your becoming a daughter-in-law in that household. They have lots of land. You would have plenty of food to eat and fancy clothes to wear. I will approach them again on the matter."

"No!" shouted Ruth. "I might have enough to eat and to wear, but I would be nothing but a slave in that family, drudging from morning until night. No, Mother. Let me make my own wedding arrangements. When I get married, I want to live in a home where I have servants to wait on me. Just give me money, and I will go to Peking where there are many wealthy families with servants. Please let me manage my own affairs."

Several weeks later Ruth set off for Peking where she bought herself gaudy clothes and found a place to live at a teahouse. Painted, perfumed, and persuasive, she soon learned from the other girls how to ply the trade.

When Lu-chia visited the establishment, she used

all her tricks and charms to attract him. It meant nothing to her that he already had a wife and children. She would force her way into his home and, if necessary, drive the first wife away and take possession of the children.

Lu-chia walked into the trap like the unwary fly into the spider's web. Since many Chinese gentlemen had more than one wife, Lu-chia did not hesitate to marry Ruth. He took her to his home to live. From the first appearance in the home, Ruth became a virtual dictator, making life intolerable for the first wife. Painted like Jezebel and dressed daily in her gaudy clothing, she ordered the meek first wife around. She would stay in bed until nearly noon while the other wife washed the clothes, cooked the food, and cleaned the house. Sitting in a carved chair smoking one cigarette after another, she gave harsh orders; and when they were not carried out to suit her, she would scream, "I'll kill you if you don't do as I say." Lu-chia often joined Ruth in screaming at the first wife and would threaten to kick her with his hobnailed boots if she did not conform to Ruth's wishes.

Together they made life unbearable for the poor woman. Their callous merriment drove her to distraction. She became so unnerved that she lost control of her bodily functions. This made her the butt of even more cruel remarks and ridicule. Finally, Lu-chia made arrangements for her to marry another man from a poorer home. And since Ruth could not have children, the two he had by the first wife became Ruth's.

By 1931 the Japanese were actively infiltrating Manchuria, intending to occupy all of that territory so rich in natural resources. Student demonstrations throughout China put pressure on President Chiang Kai-shek to make war on Japan. But he knew that China was hopelessly unprepared. His successful

Northern Expedition had brought a semblance of unity to the nation, but powerful warlords threatened the fragile peace. The new central government which had been expending its strength in the internal reconstruction and development of the country, had no capability to mobilize its armies for waging full-scale war with an outside enemy.

Then on September 18, 1931, the Japanese, who had bombed and killed the Young Marshall's father General Chang Tso-lin three years earlier, attacked Mukden, and extended their control over Manchuria. Japan appointed Henry P'u Yi, son of the last emperor of the overthrown Ching Dynasty, as the puppet ruler of China's northeastern provinces. The nation was outraged. The Young Marshall, supported by students, agitated all over the country for immediate war with Japan. But President Chiang consistently refused to declare war, knowing that his troops were no match for the crack Japanese army. Moreover, he had set as his government's first priority the elimination of domestic enemies — bandits, warlords, and communists — not foreign enemies. Chiang transferred the Young Marshall and his troops to northwest China where he would be far away from Manchuria and those who were inciting him to avenge his father's death. Lu-chia and many other Manchurian soldiers went along in the move.

When the Young Marshall continued to agitate for a united program of resistance against Japan, the President, in December, 1936, flew from the capital in Nanking to Sian for talks with him.

The Young Marshall seized the opportunity and imprisoned Chiang in one of the caves south of Sian in an attempt to force him to declare war on Japan. The whole nation and, in fact, the world was aghast at the temerity of the Young Marshall. He appeared to be planning to take over the government of the entire country, if he could not convince the President to declare war on Japan.

Lu-chia was one of the officers assigned to guard President Chiang. He and the other guards had been instructed to be kind to their hostage and to provide him with everything he asked for. One day when Lu-chia was on guard at the entrance of the cave, he asked the President whether there was anything he would like to have.

"Yes," the distinguished prisoner replied, "I would like you to go to some church in the city and buy me a Holy Bible. I read it every day, but when I set out from Nanking, I did not plan to be away long and left my Bible at home."

Lu-chia let others guard the cave while he rode his bicycle into the city to find a Bible. He inquired where he could find a church and eventually made his way to a Christian bookroom operated beside the church.

"Give me a Holy Bible," he commanded in his most dictatorial voice.

"What kind do you want?" asked the surprised and frightened attendant.

"Let me see what kinds you have," he ordered.

The clerk showed him several sizes of print and different bindings. Lu-chia looked at the inside carefully. He had never seen nor heard of a Bible before, so he really didn't know what he was looking for.

In a rage he handed the books back to the attendant shouting, "Take these back and give me a Holy Bible. These are not Holy Bibles."

The clerk had had previous experience with the violent tempers of Manchurian soldiers and went out of his way to show proper respect to Lu-chia.

"I guarantee that these are Holy Bibles. I sell many of them every day," he said calmly.

"Can't you read the title of the book?" Lu-chia

fired back. "'New and Old Testament Complete Book' is what it says. I was asked to find a Holy Bible and not this New and Old Testament thing. Get a Holy Bible for me at once or I'll make you wish you had."

"Please take one of these to the friend who sent you," the clerk replied quietly eyeing the soldier's heavy boots. "If this is not what he wants, return it to me and I will refund your money."

(At that time the Chinese Bible was called New and Old Testament Complete Book. More recently some editions have begun to use Holy Bible.)

Still fuming about the inefficiency of some clerks, Lu-chia took the book and started back to the camp on his bicycle.

He delivered the Bible in person to the President happy to learn from him that he had brought the right book.

President Chiang took the Bible, and according to old Chinese custom, began reading it aloud in his cave. Lu-chia stood as close to the entrance of the cave as possible so that he could hear what this strange book was all about. He could not understand why the President closed his eyes and knelt in prayer each day.

One day just before Christmas, as President Chiang, according to his regular custom, was reading the Bible early in the morning, he called out to Lu-chia, "Madame Chiang will be here today."

"How do you know that?" asked Lu-Chia.

"I read it in the Bible," the President replied. "Come here and read it for yourself."

Intrigued, Lu-chia read the passage to which the President was pointing, Jeremiah 31:22: "For the Lord has created a new thing on the earth: a woman protects a man."

In an hour or more they all heard the drone of a plane overhead and soon learned that it was the

President's plane bringing Madame Chiang and other top government officials for negotiations with the Young Marshall. The President was released on Christmas Day, 1936.

When the Young Marshall accompanied Chiang back to Nanking, the group that had formed his personal bodyguard was disbanded. Lu-chia was left without appointment. Suddenly his world had come tumbling down and all those dreams of serving his country as a soldier were smashed.

Lu-chia slowly returned to his senses. He went to the army barracks, picked up what belonged to him, and set out for the hotel — his only home. No longer able to rely on the Young Marshall for his livelihood, he did not know where he would turn.

Meanwhile, back at the hotel which she helped to operate, Ruth had heard newsboys shouting, "Extra! extra!" and learned the news of the release of the President. She smoked one cigarette after another as she waited nervously for word from or about her husband. When he came walking into their room at the hotel, she was wise enough not to scold him for having had part in the disgraceful capturing of the President. Lu-chia made the simple announcement, "I am through with the army. From today on I am a civilian and we will have to earn our living the best way possible."

He had saved enough money during the past years to build a home for his mother, his brother, and his own family in a growing city some miles away. Lu-chia knew that war between China and Japan was inevitable and he wanted to live in a place where there would be little danger of bombings. He and Ruth divided their time between the hotel and this home, and his children were cared for by his mother at the home when he and Ruth lived at the hotel. When business was slack, he would sit in a comfortable chair at the entrance of the hotel reading a newspaper or watching the crowds pass by.

One evening as he was sitting in his chair alongside the street, he saw an unusual sight. An attractive young woman came walking down the street leading a blind man. Lu-chia was careful about addressing strange women, but this combination so intrigued him that, as the two passed, he called to them, "Where are you going?"

The young woman replied in dignified Pekinese, "This man is a talented musician. We are on our way to the Christian church where he will play. Come along and hear him."

This aroused Lu-chia's curiosity and, before he realized what he was doing, he followed them down the street. He had never seen a blind man play an instrument. He followed them into the church — the first time he had ever entered one.

The blind man took his place at the organ and began playing beautiful Christian music. Lu-chia sat there and listened enthralled. Then the young woman stepped to the platform with a Bible in her hand and began to preach. She had not told Lu-chia that there would be preaching, or he might not have attended. She spoke about the universality of sin and about Christ the Savior of the world. Lu-chia had never heard anything like it before.

When the sermon ended, the young woman gave an invitation for anyone who felt his need of Christ to come forward and let Christ save him. Lu-chia's heart was touched. He could see sin and insecurity everywhere. Did this Christ offer a new hope? As others went forward and knelt at a wooden bench, he did the same. The lady preacher knelt in front of him.

"What is your honorable name?" she asked.

"My unworthy name is Joo," Lu-chia replied reluctantly.

"Mr. Joo, would you like to pray and confess your sins to God? You must turn to Him in repentance and have faith in our Lord Jesus."

Lu-chia had never prayed in his life nor had he ever heard clearly how anyone prayed. He recalled President Chiang praying in the cave each day. He began to confess some superficial sins. He wanted no one to know what a sinner he had been, so kept the ugly sins in his heart. He must save his face. After a few sentences of prayer, he stopped.

"How do you feel now?" asked the woman preacher.

"I feel a little better," he replied.

"A little better!" she exclaimed. "That will never do. You must get complete deliverance. The Bible says, 'He who conceals his transgressions will not prosper, but he who confesses and forsakes them will obtain mercy.' When you confess all of the sins that you can recall, God will forgive you. Then you will feel not just a little better; you will really be set free. May I pray for you?"

He listened carefully as she prayed, "O Lord! have mercy on Mr. Joo. He is a sinner. Forgive his sins as you have promised and write his name in the Lamb's Book of Life in heaven."

Lu-chia began to squirm. He had lied to her. He was not Mr. Joo. What if God wrote down the wrong name in heaven?

He reached out and tapped the preacher on the shoulder while she continued to pray, and said, "Pardon me, I lied to you. My name is not Mr. Joo. It is Mr. Sung. Please pray for me that God will forgive my sins."

After she finished praying, the preacher asked Lu-chia to pray again and confess every sin he could recall. This time with tears, he confessed his adultery, his cruelty to his first wife, his dishonesty —

everything he could recall. He poured them out before the Lord. Christ came into his troubled heart and calmed the storm. Lu-chia knew that Christ had made "all things new." At the close of the service, he arose and told others present what God had done. He was sure that God had transformed him.

When he returned to the hotel, Lu-chia told Ruth what had happened. "Tonight I followed a young woman from Peking who was leading a blind musician to a church and listened to him play and to her preach. I confessed my sins there, and God has changed me."

"What do you mean?" Ruth replied. "We might just as well die now. What is there to live for? What joy is there in sitting here in this quiet hotel watching each other every night? I want to have fun and enjoy other pleasures. Don't ask me to become a Christian. Why do you think I married you?"

"But faith in Jesus Christ is different from Buddhism," Lu-chia replied quietly. "It isn't escape from life. Jesus said, 'I have come that you may have life, and have it to the full.' That's what happened to me tonight. In the Christian religion each person believes for himself. People are not saved by families, but by individuals. If you want to remain a Buddhist, that is your privilege. But I intend to be a Christian."

Ruth went to bed troubled. From now on their family life would be different. How could she live? Now that he had become a Christian, she and Lu-chia would have nothing in common.

The next day Lu-chia hunted up the Christian bookroom where he had previously bought the Bible for President Chiang and bought one for himself. He realized that if he was to be a Christian, he would need to study the Bible to find out the Christian way of life. The clerk instructed him to begin to read from the Old Testament each morning and from the New

Testament each evening. He followed these instructions. Ruth listened intently to him as he read aloud, but she did not want him to know that she was interested. As he read the Bible aloud each day, she busied herself either dusting or sewing in the same room so that she could catch every word.

One day Lu-chia stopped in the middle of his reading. "I am beginning to get this book straight in my own mind," he announced. "The Old Testament tells about Jehovah. The New Testament tells about Jesus. They are Father and Son. Both the names begin with "Je" which must be the family surname put at the beginning of the name. So it is all about the family of God."

Lu-chia's whole life seemed to be transformed. Ruth tried to needle him in one way or another to test whether he was genuinely changed or not. After Lu-chia finished reading his Bible each day, he customarily wrapped it in a square white silk scarf and set it carefully on the table. One day Ruth was unusually cantankerous. In a rage, because he had not retaliated, she walked to the table, picked up his Bible, and hurled it across the room. It landed in a corner. He looked at her in surprise. If it had happened before he became a Christian, he would have kicked her angrily with his heavy leather boots. She waited to see how Lu-chia would react. He didn't say a word, but walked across the room, picked up the Bible and replaced it on the table. Ruth knew now that the change was genuine.

From that day forward, Ruth longed to be a Christian, to find peace with God. She mulled over the question of whether she should go with her husband to the church services. She was an inveterate smoker and bought her cigarettes in several-carton quantities. She had bought a fresh supply just before Lu-chia was saved. Now she was the only one using them. She was reluctant to throw them away and waste the money.

One day she confided her thoughts to her daughter, who was then a grown-up young woman. The daughter recommended that she hurry and smoke all of the cigarettes and then become a Christian.

"But," said Ruth, "the trouble is that I hate the sight of them. I feel less and less inclined to smoke each day."

A few weeks later Ruth decided to go with her husband to church whether the cigarettes were finished or not. After attending only a few services, she sought and found the Lord. This made a complete transformation in her life and in their home. Both Lu-chia and Ruth went around the house or the hotel singing hymns that they learned at the church. His elderly mother, his brother, and his two children also became followers of Christ.

The chain of God's faithfulness is forged link by link with His providential acts in our lives. So it was in 1940 when the Lord led James and me to leave our four children at the coast and open new work in northwest China. When we were unable to find a house, Lu-chia and Ruth kindly received us into a room in their home to live rent-free for nearly a year. It was in this room that the first services were held during those turbulent months leading up to Japan's attack on Pearl Harbor, and it was here that many souls found the Lord.

Week after week Ruth invited the wife of her husband's partner in the operation of the hotel to attend the services, but she consistently refused. She was always courteous in her refusal, but she would not come. Finally, one Sunday afternoon she appeared along with many others at Lu-chia's home.

While I was preaching that afternoon, Ruth suddenly became much disturbed and began to weep. She called out, "Please wait. I must confess my sin.

When my husband and I came as refugees to the northwest we left all of our household things behind. You all know that I like to have pretty things around in my home. As soon as we reached here we had to buy new household necessities for the whole house. I tried unsuccessfully to buy a fine tea set consisting of tray, teapot, and teacups, but none was available. All I could find were of the coarsest material and looked ugly. I know it is wartime and we all have to do without luxuries, but I was determined that I would have a set of fine tea service to use when friends visited. The wife of my husband's partner kindly offered to lend me a set that she had until I could buy one for myself. Her set is still here in my home where I use it every day. I have not looked for a set since she lent this set to me. I have looked upon her set as my own and have not thought of returning it to her.

"Mrs. Chang, can you ever forgive me for my covetousness? How wrong I have been! Will you please forgive? I will return your beautiful set today." Ruth knelt before her friend:

Mrs. Chang took her by the hand and said, "Please arise. I forgive you. But I must say that I have wondered how anyone could be such a devout Christian and not return someone else's borrowed property. Now I know that you are genuine. From my heart I forgive you."

At the close of the message that day, Mrs. Chang herself knelt and sought the Lord. He came into her heart. Just as the Bible promises, when Christians walk in the light, they have fellowship with one another, and the blood of Jesus purifies from every sin. When Mrs. Chang returned to her home that afternoon, she not only had Christ in her heart, but she was also carrying her precious tea set, tied in a cloth in her hand.

Ruth loved to keep her home immaculately clean.

She swept and dusted every part of her house every day. One day when I invited her to go calling in homes with me, she replied, "I am too busy. I have to clean my house." Later the Lord rebuked her, and she knelt and confessed that she loved cleanliness more than she loved souls. Thereafter she frequently accompanied me when I called in homes.

Ruth's voice could be heard each morning before others were out of bed as she prayed earnestly for those around her. She did house-to-house visitation and won many to her Christ. Lu-chia and Ruth's big regret was that they had not met Christ sooner before they had wrecked the first wife's life. It was a joy to visit their home where Christ was the theme of their conversation and where they always wanted to delve deeper into the truths of the Bible.

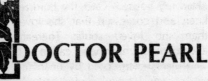

Chapter Three

DOCTOR PEARL

SALVATION IN EXCHANGE FOR A SQUASH

Who can that refined and attractive lady be that is giving such close attention to the sermon? thought my husband as he was preaching one Sunday morning in northwest China.

It was not good Chinese custom for a man to talk to a strange woman, especially when his own wife was not present. But since this was obviously an educated woman, he felt that she might be more modern in her outlook on old customs. At the close of the service, as my husband stood at the door of the church, he welcomed her to the church and invited her to come to our home and meet me when she could find opportunity. Tears filled the young woman's eyes as she received this invitation. She promised to pay a visit soon.

A few days later, having returned from an evangelistic tour in the countryside, I was sitting in our home, when I saw the well-dressed young woman coming to the door. As she entered, I noticed that she was carrying a very unusual variety of squash. "I am Dr. Pearl," she said introducing herself. We have some very rare squashes growing on an arbor in our yard, and I wanted to bring this big one especially for you." (In China it is a common custom to take a gift when calling on someone.) The squash had four perfect white lobes that looked like four unbaked raised buns suspended from the bottom of the golden squash.

After thanking her and discussing the squash for a short time, I asked, "Dr. Pearl, are you a Christian?"

"Let me tell you my story," she replied as tears came to her eyes. "My parents were both earnest Christians. In fact, they dedicated all of us brothers and sisters to the Lord in our infancy. From my earliest childhood, I went to Sunday school regularly. After finishing high school I decided that I wanted to become a doctor so that I could relieve some of China's suffering. I went to Peking and entered the Peking Union Medical College where I graduated as a doctor of medicine.

"It was while studying there that I met Mr. Lew, a widower with two daughters who was very much in love with me and begged me to marry him. He had grown up steeped in Chinese traditional religions. I knew that I should not marry a non-Christian, because the Bible clearly teaches that believers should not be yoked together with unbelievers. However, I justified my actions by saying that I would do all in my power to win him and his family to the Lord. I would accept his home as my mission field. Against my parents' advice and protests, I married Mr. Lew. But he has never been interested in my Christian faith and has consistently refused to attend any church services with me. Gradually, I became very cold toward God until I even thought that God no longer wants me.

"When the advancing Japanese troops began to threaten our town in north China, my husband's whole family and I fled and finally settled here. We thought we might escape bombings in this remote place. But even here, as you know, we have frequent air raid warnings.

"Two weeks ago when the air raid siren sounded, as many of us as could fled to the fields. Some got on bicycles and sped to the hills farther away from town. I had only got as far as a cornfield on the outskirts of the town when I heard the ominous drone of the bombers approaching overhead. The shrieking of sirens in town warned everyone to freeze where he was and not move. I fell on my face in the cornfield.

"A Christian woman kneeling on the ground a few feet from me began to pray aloud earnestly asking God to protect all of us. Suddenly I heard a shrill, sickening whistle and an enormous thud just in front of us. Mud and cornstalks flew in every direction. Bombs began exploding some distance away. Then there was silence. Trembling, I opened my eyes to see what it was that had struck so close with such impact. We found that a bomb had buried itself deep in the center of the cornfield. It had not exploded!

"The Christian woman exclaimed, 'Just see! God has heard our prayer and spared our lives.' I was all shaken up and decided then and there that I would get back to God. Though I was deliberately going against Him, He had miraculously spared my rebellious life. True to my promise, last Sunday I went to church. Your husband saw me and invited me to come to see you. That is why I am here today."

I shared with Dr. Pearl her joy in God's wonderful mercy to her. Then I reminded her of God's promise to the people of Israel when they backslid. I told her how He had said in II Chronicles 7:14, "If my people who are called by my name will humble themselves and pray, and seek my face and turn from their wicked ways, then I will hear from heaven, will forgive their sin, and will heal their land." After examining a few other Bible promises, we knelt together in prayer before the Lord, and God graciously gave her the kiss of forgiveness and restored to her the joys of salvation. She came with a squash in her hand, but went away with God's salvation in her heart.

Dr. Pearl bought a Bible so that she could read it in her spare time. Often she would leave it lying on the table in the waiting room so that patients could read it as they waited their turn to see the doctor. From that day forward she became an active participant in all the services of the local church, even though her husband still refused to go along. The doctor encouraged her two daughters, who were students in the local high school, to attend the young people's services of the church. Before long, they, too, became Christians.

One day weeks later my husband and I called in the home and met the seventy-five-year-old mother-in-law. I explained to her in minute detail how, in the beginning, man had fallen and how God had sent His Son to redeem fallen man. She was attentive to all we said. The Lord opened old Mrs. Lew's heart to respond to our message. It was the first time she had heard the gospel. I knelt with her on the large flat brick bed as she prayed and asked Christ to save her. Since she had never attended school and could neither read nor write, it was remarkable how much of our talk she had absorbed.

She prayed intelligently, confessing her sins and asking God to free her from them. Among other things she said, "O God, when I was fifteen years old, I was married and went to live at my husband's home. One of the first tasks that was assigned to me was to take my mother-in-law's long bamboo-stemmed brass pipe many times a day, fill it with tobacco, light it, and return it to her to smoke. Of course, I had to take a few puffs on it to get the tobacco in the bowl lighted. It was not long until I found that I, too, had acquired the smoking habit. For sixty years my pipe has been my constant companion. Now, Lord, please set me free from it. I want only the things that you want me to have. Please take this filthy habit from me."

It was a delight to see joy from above fill her heart and shine out on that dark face marred by years of sin and idolatry. Going over to a table near the bed, she gathered up her cigarettes and brass pipe and destroyed them immediately, exclaiming, "Now that I have Jesus, I won't need them anymore." And she didn't need them. God had given Grandma Lew a deeper satisfaction.

Several days later, the young servant in the home who understood nothing of the power of Christ, felt that the missionary was cheating the old lady out of a pleasure that she should have. According to Chinese custom, the elderly should be granted their every wish, if possible, and especially be pampered as old age advances. The servant had never known of anyone who had broken the smoking habit and was sure that the old lady must be suffering intensely because of having stopped smoking so abruptly.

Coming to her in the courtyard one day he said, "Grandma, don't let that missionary cheat you out of your pleasure. You have smoked all of your life and must not think of trying to break off now. You must have suffered terribly these last few days."

"No, I haven't," she replied, "I not only have not suffered nor desired to smoke, but now it even nauseates me to smell someone else smoking."

He protested, "You can't fool me. You have smoked for sixty years, and can't possibly break off without extreme discomfort. Let me go and light a pipe and bring it to you. I want to see you enjoying your pipe again."

"No, I don't want any more tobacco," she replied, "Christ has set me free."

He persisted, trying to gain her consent. She was just as persistent in declining. In the end, however, he filled and lit a pipe and brought it to her.

"Now, smoke this," he said.

"No," she kept protesting, "I tell you I don't want it any more. I don't want to taste the stuff ever again."

But he became even more insistent. He put the lighted pipe to her lips and said, "Here it is. Now smoke this and don't be cheated out of your lifelong pleasure any more."

To pacify him in his persistence and to get rid of him, Grandma Lew took a puff. Immediately her head began to swim. She felt as though she was going to faint. Quickly she supported herself by leaning against the wall and only in this way was able to keep from falling down.

"Help me into the house," she called. "I told you I didn't want it. Now it has made me sick." He supported her as she went inside and got up onto her bed. After a good night's sleep, she was all right again.

Later in recounting this episode to me she said, "Through this experience God showed me that He had really set me free from the habit. After that no one has ever tried to offer a pipe to me again."

Because she had tiny bound feet, Grandma Lew usually did not travel far from home. Walking on bound feet was painful but after she found Christ, she began to come to all of the services at the church a half mile from her home. She gradually unbound her feet which relieved some of the pain when she walked. But because in her girlhood they had broken the bones of her feet when they bound them, she never could go entirely without the long bandages to hold the bones in place when she walked.

She attended the class for baptism at the church and when asked what mode of baptism she wanted, she replied, "I want to be immersed. I don't want any little wash."

Baptisms were to be held in the early spring. The weather on that high plateau was still very cold. The brick baptistry was in an open courtyard behind the church. Dr. Pearl suggested that her mother-in-law ought to be sprinkled, as she feared she might develop pneumonia if she were immersed in cold water in the open air. But Grandma Lew knew exactly what she wanted. She would be immersed.

Secretly she brought a change of clothing and a towel to church, preparing for immersion. As she stepped down into the baptistry, the minister paused to make a brief prayer for her. Thinking that he was intending only to sprinkle her, she sat down in the water and began splashing water all over her shoulders and head. When the prayer was finished, the minister quickly realized that if he didn't go ahead and immerse Grandma Lew, she was going to do it herself. When he completed the ceremony she announced triumphantly, "I wanted only the type of baptism that Jesus had. I wouldn't let them trick me into accepting anything less."

God used Dr. Pearl and her family to bring many friends and relatives in that town to the Lord. She used every opportunity to tell others of Christ's power to save. Grandma Lew also continued to witness to God's transforming power as she went from home to home urging others to believe in the Christ who had done so much for her.

. . . . .

One Saturday evening at the close of a young people's service Dr. Pearl arose and made special request. "I want to ask prayer for a relative of mine who lives here in town," she said. "He has been a corrupt government official and now is nearing the end as a result of his immoral ways. Outside of God there is no hope for him. Please help me pray for him."

The service was dismissed and all went to their homes. But that night I could not sleep for thinking of the dying official who did not know God.

Sunday afternoon I went to Pastor Mark's home and asked if he would like to go with me to see Mr. Chang. He, too, had been praying for his salvation. Together we rode our bicycles to the home, with Dr. Pearl leading the way. When we came into the courtyard, many relatives and friends were huddled together talking in subdued voices. Mr. Chang, racked with disease, had become violent and, locking himself in his house, would let no one enter. In fact, if anyone even went to the window to try to talk with him, he would tear bricks out of his bed and throw them. Understandably, everyone was keeping a safe distance.

Dr. Pearl quietly introduced us to Mr. Chang's wife and the friends in the yard and told them the reason for our visit. All shook their heads and let us know he was beyond help. His mind was gone. It would only be a matter of time until the disease had taken its toll and he would be gone.

But we knew that God had sent us. Praying silently for protection, I walked up to the barred window and called, "Mr. Chang, we have come from the Christian church to pray for you. Jesus is able to make you well. Please open the door and let us come in."

"What did you say?" he asked.

Again I repeated what I had said, "We are here to help you. Please open the door and let us come in."

"Wait until I get dressed," he replied rationally. "Please come in," he called to us in a few minutes as he opened the door.

Pastor Mark and I entered and sat down beside Mr. Chang on the remains of his brick bed. We began to tell him of the true God who is different from the idols that he had worshiped all of his life. They are the work of men's hands. They have mouths, but they cannot speak; they have eyes, but they cannot see; they have ears, but they cannot hear; they have hands, but they cannot help; they have feet, but they cannot walk. Those who make them become like them. The true God, however, loved him and sent His Son to die for his sins.

Mr. Chang had never heard of Jesus and found it difficult to comprehend all that we were saying. Though he was an educated man, he was now in a deplorable state. The portions of the brain that control vision had already been affected by the ravages of his disease. Urging him to think over what we had told him, and encouraging him to turn to the living God, we left. We promised to return the following day.

Mr. Chang and his wife welcomed us the next afternoon as we arrived. He remembered what we had told him the previous day and wanted to hear more. Again the four of us sat on the half-destroyed brick bed as we talked to them about repentance and faith in Jesus Christ. We then described His gracious invitation, "Behold, I stand at the door and knock; if anyone hears my voice and opens the door, I will come in to him, and will eat with him, and he with me" (Revelation 3:19 RSV). Before we left that afternoon, both Mr. Chang and his wife prayed asking God's forgiveness and inviting Jesus to come into their hearts. And come in He did.

A few days later a group of Christians went with us for a short service in the home as they took down their idols and burned them in the courtyard. Though Mr. Chang could not see to read and his wife was illiterate, he bought a Bible for his son, who was in high school, to read to them. Every day he and his wife prayed together. They often asked visitors to read from their Bible for them. They began attending all of the church services regularly, and their spiritual progress was most gratifying to see. Mr. Chang began praying that since God had forgiven his sins he would also restore his vision to him so that he could read his Bible.

One winter day as he sat out in the warm sunshine in the courtyard with his Bible in his lap, he opened it to see if he could read anything.

"Wife, come here," he called. "I can see. Come and hear me read." She came running to his side and sat there while he read chapter after chapter.

Christ came to mean everything to both of them.

One day Mrs. Chang came to our home to ask if someone could come to pray for their seven-year-old grandson, who had been critically ill for several days. The doctor had diagnosed the illness as polio and had predicted that the child would never be able to walk again or at best would be pitifully crippled.

"Can Jesus heal him?" Mrs. Chang asked.

We went with her and laying hands on the child, prayed that Jesus, who is "the same yesterday, today, and forever," would draw near and bring healing to him. Then we went on our way. The next day when we called to ask how the child was, she said, "Didn't we ask Jesus to heal him? Well, He did it. This morning when our grandson arose, he was well. The temperature was gone and he felt fine. He has gone off to school." From that day forward the lad lived a normal life with no crippling effects.

That spring both Mr. and Mrs. Chang were baptized and joined the church. God had restored his mind enough so that he could grasp the way of salvation and read the Word. Still there were days of weakness and times of testing.

One afternoon that fall, Mrs. Chang came to our home very much disturbed. While she had gone to the market to buy some provisions, Mr. Chang, whose mind had slipped again, had walked out of the yard and down the street, unnoticed. As soon as she returned home and found that he was gone, she came to the church, asking us to pray that she might know which direction to take in order to find him. He could have gone in any of the four directions and walked out of a city gate.

After prayer, Mrs. Chang felt that she should go out the west gate and ask if anyone had seen her husband. A cart driver whom she met on the road told her that he had seen a man who matched her description walking westward. On she went trying to find him. Darkness forced her to go to an inn for the night.

At daybreak she started out again and had gone only a short distance when she was impressed to follow north outside the city wall. There, almost in sight of the main road, her husband lay. Someone had stolen his woolen cap and warm shoes, but otherwise he was all right. Mrs. Chang hired a horse cart to take him home, where she kept close watch thereafter lest he run away again.

One afternoon after she had escorted a caller to the front gate, she returned to their room to find that Mr. Chang was dying. She became frightened. She had never seen a Christian die, but she had seen many heathen die. In their anguish they would often cry out, "Save me! Save me! The evil spirits have come for me!" Though her husband had labored breathing, he was calm and peaceful with a smile on his face. Often heathen relatives leave the room when a loved one dies so that they do not hear his cries. Mrs. Chang waited to see what would happen. A peaceful smile passed over his face, and his breathing stopped. He had gone to be with Jesus.

She came to the church to tell us and to ask how Christians are buried. Through her tears she exclaimed, "He is gone. But it was wonderful. If people received nothing from believing in Jesus but to have such peace when they die, it is worth it all. But besides that we have hope of heaven and Jesus throughout all eternity."

Some months later Mrs. Chang came to our home to make a friendly visit and have prayer together. When she saw me, she exclaimed, "Why are you looking so pale? You look ghastly. What is wrong?"

I replied, "I have been doing some difficult traveling recently which has necessitated walking over long, rough roads in the rains, climbing steep, slippery banks, and fording rivers that were so swift that it was necessary for the gospel team to hold hands while we waded across, lest we be swept down the river and drowned. As a result I have developed the same trouble as the woman who came and touched the hem of Christ's garment."

"Have you prayed about it?" she asked earnestly.

I had to admit that I had not, but had just hoped that the trouble would clear up. "Would you pray for me, please, Mrs. Chang?" I asked.

"All right," she answered. "I'll pray for you when I get home."

"No," I said. "Please pray for me right now."

"I don't know how to make a pretty prayer in public," she replied.

"God doesn't want to hear a pretty prayer," I said. "He likes a prayer of faith that comes from the heart. Shall we kneel together and you pray right here for me?"

As we knelt, this dear illiterate Christian sister closed her eyes and said, "Now Lord, Mrs. Taylor is sick and has little strength for the work she has to do. Please lay Your hand upon her and make her well right now. I thank You, Lord. In Jesus' name, Amen."

As we arose from our knees, I knew my trouble was ended. It never returned.

Mrs. Chang continued to have great faith for

healing and also for the salvation of souls. She was able to lead her children and grandchildren to the Lord. She had the simple, trusting faith of a little child.

Chapter Four

DOCTOR CHIU

HE DISCOVERED TRUE HEALING

As he made his rounds of the wards, the efficient young medic found it difficult to concentrate on his patients. The morning paper that day had described the ominous westward advance of the invading Japanese armies. In a startling move, the government had cut the dikes of the Yellow River, stopping the enemy's armored divisions in their tracks. But as the swirling waters of "China's Sorrow" found their new course, thousands had been drowned and hundreds of thousands made homeless.

Added to all this was the report of immense areas of north China suffering from drought and now in terrible famine condition. Trees were being stripped of their bark and roots dug up as starving peasants foraged for food.

But what troubled Dr. Chiu more as he moved from ward to ward was a deep sense of anguish and indignation that burned within him. He thought of the plight of his country in the face of such natural disaster and the enemy's inhumanity. Shot through with corruption and self-seeking, the government and military were impotent to heal the wounds of a nation that was slowly bleeding to death.

That day the young medic resolved that he would do something about it. He dug out his college textbook on the Confucian classics. For centuries the

57

path to political service had been through the study of these revered texts. Surely they bore the answer to China's woes.

Night after night when his rounds were completed, Dr. Chiu poured over the Confucian Analects, The Doctrine of the Mean, Mencius and the other ancient classics. With no electricity, he read by the light of a tiny peanut oil lamp on his table.

Yet, as he read, there was a nagging question that troubled Dr. Chiu. If correct teaching and right relationships, as Confucius had emphasized, provided the answer he sought for China, why had others not found it and applied the proscription long ago?

He broadened his reading to include the writing of the Legalists. Those ancient philosophers had influenced Emperor Chin Shih, the great unifier of China who lived 220 B. C. They insisted that human nature is basically evil and teaching is not enough. Their proscription was an intricate system of rewards and punishments. Severe penalites would discourage people from wrong doing, and corruption would be stamped out.

"If a few heads are chopped off," the young medic thought, "is that the place to begin? Among my friends and associates, there are also those who have broken the law. Even I myself am not free from evil. Where is the answer to the renewal of our sick society? Where will China turn for salvation?"

As these thoughts surged through his mind, Dr. Chiu's memory carried him back to a passing remark his cousin had made years before. While in high school his cousin had once invited him to go to church. "All they do is preach about sin," he remembered him saying. Chiu had declined. He wasn't interested in any foreign religion.

But now that comment came back to him. "All they do is preach about sin." "If they preach about sin, then surely they must have a remedy for it," the medic thought. "I wonder what it is."

The leather-bound book lying on the table in the waiting room of Dr. Pearl's office caught Dr. Chiu's eye.

What is this well-bound medical book? he thought as he picked it up. He was visiting Dr. Pearl, a refugee friend originally from the same area of Japanese-occupied China. *During these war times we do not often see such fine bindings as this,* he mused.

"Holy Bible," he read on the cover. *This must be a Christian Bible,* he thought. Opening it, he began to read in Genesis and was fascinated. He had never read such true-to-life stories. Every chapter seemed to be directed right to his heart.

"Where did you get this book?" he asked Dr. Pearl when she finally came into the room.

"I bought it at the Christian church last week when I was over there," she replied.

"Do they have any more like it?" he asked. "Would they sell me a copy? Do they sell to people who are not Christians? It's interesting that only recently I was thinking about a book that would describe the Christian religion for me."

"The Bible will certainly do that. I will see if I can get one for you," Dr. Pearl replied. "However, Bibles are hard to obtain now that the war is on. No one is allowed to transport them across enemy lines. The church has even been restricting the sale of its limited supply to one copy per Christian family."

Later, when Dr. Pearl came to our home, she was so convincing in her assurance that Dr. Chiu would read the Bible that we sold her a copy. A few days later she escorted us to the branch hospital where Dr. Chiu was in charge to see how he was progressing with his Bible reading and to tell him how he might find Christ. We were surprised to find that he had already completed almost half of the Old Testament and much of the New Testament. He asked penetrating, intelligent questions indicating that God was speaking personally to his heart through the Word. We invited him to come to our home the following day for further discussion.

When he arrived, Dr. Chiu was carrying his precious Bible in a white silk kerchief. He had also sewed white silk cloth over the covers to preserve the Bible from the hard wear which he would give it. I shall never forget the scene. There in the quiet of our living room we told Dr. Chiu how to give his heart to God.

Though he was a successful doctor with a good education, he was not offended by the simplicity of the message; and when we asked him to pray, he poured out his soul to God in great earnestness and complete sincerity. And God heard him. His face radiated the joy of the Lord as he arose from his knees. He believed I John 1:9, "If we confess our sins, He is faithful and just to forgive us our sins and to cleanse us from all unrighteousness." That day he became a child of God. Never before had he experienced anything like it. He had made a vital contact with the living God, and was prepared in a new way to serve his country.

Dr. Chiu lived only a block from the Northwest Bible Institute that had just opened for the purpose of training young people for Christian service. As soon as he was saved, he began attending student prayers morning and evening at the Bible school. When the new semester opened, he applied for admission as a student. It was possible for him to choose courses in such a way so that it did not conflict with his hospital duties and care of patients. He was able to carry a full load of classes at the Bible Institute. How he enjoyed delving daily into the Word of God with experienced teachers to help open up new truths to him! It was remarkable how he was able to keep up with his studies and still give adequate care to the patients in the hospital. An orderly would come for him in case of an emergency.

Late one cold winter afternoon a springless wooden-wheeled horse cart stopped outside the admission entrance of Dr. Chiu's branch hospital and discharged a very sick passenger. Orderlies carried the sick man into the emergency room. When the young medic came in to examine him, with great effort and labored breathing the patient said, "I am Colonel Su from your home province. I have been critically ill for days. I am sure that you will do all you can to save my life."

After examination and tests Dr. Chiu realized that the colonel was suffering from an acute case of appendicitis. His appendix could rupture at any moment. The branch hospital did not have facilities for surgery. Nor of course were antibiotics developed as they are today. Another ride by horse cart to the larger base hospital over rough and rutted roads would certainly prove fatal.

As the colonel's temperature continued to rise, he lapsed into a coma. Nothing that Dr. Chiu prescribed now seemed to have any effect. From the irregular pulse, he realized that his patient's heart was failing. The colonel was dying. What more could he do?

Slowly, with a despairing heart, he returned to his quarters. As he entered his office he saw his silk-covered Bible lying on the desk.

I will read some of this for comfort, he thought. *Many times when I have been in a quandary I have found help here.*

Dr. Chiu's daily reading was in the book of Hebrews. As he reached the thirteenth chapter and the eighth verse he came to abrupt attention. "Jesus Christ

is the same yesterday and today and forever."
"Yesterday and today and forever," he mused.
Yesterday He performed many miracles while He was
here on earth. Even after He had ascended to heaven,
through His followers, Jesus performed miracles and
healed all kinds of diseases. I wonder if He ever cured
a patient with appendicitis? If He is the same today as
yesterday, He certainly can do it. I will put Him to the
test!"

Closing his Bible, the Christian medic knelt on the
brick floor of his office and with deep emotion prayed.
"O Lord, Your Word tells me that Jesus Christ is the
same yesterday and today and forever. I have read
how You healed all kinds of diseases when You were
here upon earth. You even brought the dead back to
life. There is a desperately sick patient in this hospital
who has parents, a wife, and two children dependent
upon him. I have completely exhausted all my
medical skill, but still he is dying. Lord, please lay
Your hand upon him just as You did for others when
You were here on earth. I have never asked You to
heal a patient before, but I believe You can. I am
testing You. But let it be for Your glory and honor.
Please hear my prayer. In the name of Jesus. Amen."

Dr. Chiu felt comforted as he arose from his knees
and went about the daily routine of visting the sick in
the wards. Before long he returned to the room of
Colonel Su's. His heart beat faster as he approached
the door wondering to himself, *What will I find here?
Has Jesus heard my prayer and healed him?* He
walked into the room and felt the head and hand of
the patient; both were wet with perspiration. He felt
the pulse; the heartbeat seemed stronger and more
regular. He asked the nurse to take the colonel's
temperature; it was lower. His patient had passed the
crisis! He would live! Turning to the orderly who was
accompanying him he exclaimed, "God has answered

prayer for this man!"

His joy could scarcely be contained as he walked back to his office, *What a wonderful God we have!* he thought, *Not only can He forgive our sins and make sinners fit for heaven, but He can also heal our diseases!*

Colonel Su's recovery was rapid, and soon he was sitting in a chair wrapped in a warm quilt. One day as Dr. Chiu came into the ward, a broad smile spread over the colonel's face and he said, "Doctor, I owe my life to you. As soon as my ear catches the sound of your footsteps coming down the brick corridor, my heart is filled with a profound sense of gratitude. Before I came here I had heard of your reputation as a doctor. Now I have personally experienced your skill. You have saved my life. I will never be able to repay you for all you have done for me. How can I ever express my appreciation to you?"

It would have been easy for the doctor quietly to accept this expression of gratitude, or to take credit for the recovery, acknowledging that he had had special training when he attended medical school in Peking and had used the best modern therapy available. But he knew it was not his medical skill that had saved the dying man. He also knew the colonel had probably never heard of Jesus Christ and would not understand a medical man praying for healing. But he felt he must give God the glory and perhaps through this he might win his patient to Christ.

"Colonel, he began, "You are most generous with your words of appreciation. However, I must confess that it was not my ability or skill that saved your life. I am a worshiper of Jesus, the true God. Actually I have been a believer only a short time. When you reached the crisis shortly after you were brought in, I knew that medically there was no more we could do for you here. You were dying. It seemed that I could not bear to see your children left fatherless or your parents without care. As I returned to my room, I picked up my Bible and read the words, 'Jesus Christ is the same yesterday and today and forever.' Previously I had read how He had healed many people when He was here on earth, long ago. I knelt right there in my office and asked Him to heal you. He heard my prayer! That very day your temperature broke and your heartbeat strengthened. It was God who made you well and not I. You must thank Him and not me."

The colonel was puzzled! Thoughtfully he asked, "You say this foreign God, Jesus, made me well? I have never worshiped Him in my whole life, and yet you say He was willing to heal me? I cannot understand such love and mercy. Where can I read about Him? How should I reward Him for healing me?"

Dr. Chiu tried to tell him of God's plan of salvation and also lent him his Bible to read a short time each day as he became stronger.

"Can I believe in this Christ, too?" Colonel Su asked the doctor a few days later. "How can I worship Him who has saved my life? What can I do to find Him?"

In the best way he knew, the Christian medic shared with the officer how he had come to know the Lord. "The missionaries who brought me to Christ live just a block from here," Dr. Chiu concluded. "As soon as you are strong enough I will take you to their home and they will tell you better than I, how to find the Lord. Would you like to go?"

"I am ready to go any day," he said.

Word was sent to us that the colonel and his attendants were coming to visit. Dressed in military uniform and accompanied by his nephew and several bodyguards, he arrived at our little living room. After serving tea and cookies, we began to talk to him about how to believe in the true God. The colonel was most attentive to every word. When we asked him if he would like to let Jesus into his heart that very day, he replied, "That's what I came here for. I owe my life to Him. Even though I had never worshiped Him, He healed me. Now I want to give myself to Him."

"Are you willing to kneel before Him and confess your need of Him?" we asked.

"Yes, I am," he answered.

With that he arose, removed his officer's belt, sword, and revolver and knelt on the floor. Colonel Su wanted to come to Christ in simplicity and humility without any rank or position. He prayed a simple prayer, thanking God for healing him when he was at death's door, even though he had never worshiped Him in all his life. Then he gave himself to Christ. After a brief prayer, he turned to us and said, "He has come into my heart. I feel a deep change. From today forward I am a Christian. Now I want to lead the other members of my family and my friends to Christ."

After some urging by his uncle, the nephew also prayed and asked God to come into his heart.

Soon after his recovery Colonel Su moved his family into our community so they could attend church services. When we called in his home, his wife also accepted Christ as her Savior and was baptized with her husband. For years we watched his walk with the Lord and could see the colonel grow in grace and in the knowledge of God.

Dr. Chiu continued to attend classes in Northwest Bible Institute along with his duties at the branch hospital. Increasingly he felt a call from God to leave the medical profession and enter full-time Christian ministry. Yet, with the scarcity of trained medical personnel during the war, he realized it would take a miracle for him to get his discharge from the armed forces. Friends at church continued to pray that God would work his release. After four years of double duty as Bible school student and doctor, he again made application for discharge from military service.

At this particular time there was special need for a trained preacher to care for the church that had begun in the Chang home, where Bamboo Princess had been. The congregation had now moved to a newly constructed chapel.

Soon after Dr. Chiu was graduated from Northwest Bible Institute, his commanding officer called him into his office and said, "For several years I have been observing your unusual medical ability and have noticed that since you have become a Christian you have been doing two kinds of work: you have been performing your medical duties and have been helping men and women to adopt a high moral standard for life. This, I acknowledge, is the greatest need of our country today. Though it will be extremely difficult to find a replacement for you, I am reluctantly signing a recommendation for your discharge. The moral needs of the nation are more important than the physical. It should take about two weeks for the papers to be processed and for you to get your release."

In two weeks the papers came through. It was a great answer to prayer. What rejoicing Dr. Chiu had as he took up the pastoral care of this new church in the provincial capital!

From the time Dr. Chiu was appointed there was constant revival. The chapel was open nightly for several years and a great number of precious souls believed on Jesus. The local Christians took over full responsibility for the expenses and support of their pastor.

In a short time the church was not only self-supporting but was also giving generously to send Chinese missionaries to the unreached peoples of central Asia. They contributed regularly to the expenses of the newly organized Back-to-Jerusalem Evangelistic Band.

At the end of World War II, Dr. Chiu's wife and teenage daughter came to him from occupied territory. At first his wife wanted none of his foreign religion; the idolatrous religions of China were good enough for her. She opposed him in his preaching and forbade their daughter to attend any services.

The believers took this situation to the Lord with fasting and prayer. How could they have a pastor with a rebellious heathen wife who would try to tear down what he had built? After weeks of earnest prayer they received an answer. God put a hunger in the heart of Mrs. Chiu for the joy and peace she saw in her husband and the other Christians. When she sought God, her whole life was changed. She threw herself wholeheartedly into the work to which God had called her husband and helped him in every possible way. Their daughter also became a devout Christian. It was a delight to see the three of them combine their efforts for the upbuilding of God's kingdom in that strategic city.

JOAB

A COLONEL'S VICTORY

"Why are my men dying like flies?" Colonel Joab asked himself. "It is time I did some introspection. Is it because of some wrong that they or I have done, or something their ancestors have done, or is our country at fault? Who has the answer to these questions?"

Joab sat alone in his office and gave himself to serious reflection. What could be done to stop the toll of death that was sweeping the two battalions of troops sent so recently to that remote town in northwest China? The sick men suddenly ran high temperatures and lay in their bunks day after day until death relieved them of their misery. The colonels of the two battalions had brought in doctors of Western medicines as well as those trained in the Chinese art of acupuncture and treatment by the use of herbs. But nothing stopped the epidemic or cured the disease.

As he reflected on his past Joab wondered if there were something in his conduct that could be causing this plague to sweep through his troops as a punishment to him. He had been brought up in the old style Chinese home where his parents had engaged him to a neighbor's daughter when he was still a child. They had felt that the two families were of the same social and economic status and that they had done a good deed for their son by taking care of the biggest concern that he would have to face in life. But as he grew older and went away from home to school, he had begun to look down with disdain on his fiancée who had never attended school. Instead, with her tiny bound feet, she had sat at home all day learning to cook and sew so that when the time came for her to get married, she would know how to manage a home efficiently.

Joab, however, was planning a military career. Now it was no longer popular for a man to have an uneducated wife with bound feet. Modern women were literate and had natural feet. How could he succeed if he consented to take his neighbor's daughter for a wife? He had never seen much of her because she had been kept inside her courtyard away from the peering eyes of all men. If his parents would only consent to break this engagement and exchange her for her younger sister, he would be happy. The younger girl refused to have her feet bound and insisted that her parents permit her to attend school. She and Joab had played together many times. Something in their likes and dispositions blended perfectly.

He decided to present the proposition to his parents and to ask them to change his engagement from the older to the younger sister. But his parents were adamant. How could they go to a neighbor and tell them that they did not want their daughter, that she was not good enough for their son? It would precipitate an immediate lawsuit. Every time Joab suggested it, they flatly refused. Undaunted, he and the younger sister met secretly whenever he was home from school, making their own plans for marriage, in spite of his parents' disapproval. "Aren't modern young people choosing their own life companions today?" the young people argued.

When Joab was sixteen, his parents set the date of the wedding. He had forewarned them many times that he would never live with the older sister even though they compelled him to marry her. Because it was his filial duty, he would go through with the ceremony; but he would leave home immediately never to return. According to the custom of the community, his parents invited all the neighbors and friends to the wedding in their courtyard. The illiterate bride with her tiny bound feet was escorted into the yard and led to her place beside the groom where they made the three customary bows to his parents and to each other, which made them man and wife. Then a huge feast was served to all guests. As soon as the guests had left, Joab also left to go back to his school. Though his parents repeatedly urged him to come home, he steadfastly refused.

Secretly, he continued his correspondence with the younger sister. Several years later, she quietly left home and the two had their own wedding with his military friends. He was now well on his way to being an officer in the Chinese army and was happy because he had the wife he wanted.

But now, years later, as he thought of his dying troops, Joab wondered if his disregard for his parents' wishes could be the reason for these deaths. He had committed the sin of being unfilial, which, in Chinese eyes, is the greatest of all sins. Was the law of retribution operating?

Joab had decided to make the army a career, and one promotion after another had come his way. Before World War II, after Japan provoked war with China, at the battle of Shanghai, Joab's division had been assigned to the front lines. Bullets were flying and shells bursting all around him, while men were dying on every side. Fear gripped his heart as he wondered when his turn would come. His thoughts turned to his wife and five children, and he wondered what his wife would do to support the family if he were killed. Then a thought struck him. Everyone was so busy with his own part in the fighting that no one had time to see what others were doing. A strong urge came to Joab to do something to get away from the front lines. While no one was looking, he seized the bayonet from his gun and inflicted a deep wound on his upper leg. Immediately he was carried off the battlefield and sent to a base hospital where the self-inflicted wound was treated. After his recovery, he received a medal for bravery in action and a promotion to the rank of colonel.

He had thought that because he and his wife had been deeply in love with each other and had married from their own choice, they could never quarrel. But his was a most unhappy home. It seemed that they differed on almost every subject.

The children drove him nearly crazy. He could bear the sight of none of them, not even his eldest son. When the colonel came into the courtyard of his home, the children would run from him lest they receive a slap or a kick from him. Once when he came home for supper, he found his wife in a paroxysm of anguish, tearing at her clothes. She had taken hot wood alcohol hoping thereby to end her miserable existence. Medical help had brought her back to life, but he hated her the more for the attempt.

Added to this, their infant son had been ill for weeks and they could find no help for him. His whole body burned with a high temperature day after day until neither Joab nor his wife could get any rest. Joab had taken to sleeping in his office so as to get away from the responsibility of caring for a sick child at night. Now with his wife in anguish from attempted suicide and the baby boy showing no other sign of life than an incessant moaning, he ordered a young soldier boy to take the baby out and bury him, even though the child had not stopped breathing.

As Joab sat in his office, helpless to save the lives of his soldiers who were dying of plague, he relived these past experiences and wondered if the wickedness of his own life had anything to do with present conditions. Was it his punishment for past misdeeds?

His thoughts were interrupted by a knock on the office door. As Joab opened it, a young stranger with a happy smile greeted him, "Good evening, Colonel. May I come in? Are you busy at present? I am pastor of a Christian church fifteen miles from here. We heard that two battalions of troops are quartered in your town and decided to come here and tell these soldiers about the living God. Since you are one of their leaders I have come to see you first and to plan together where and how we can tell both officers and enlisted men about the true God. Are you a Christian, Colonel? Have you heard of Jesus Christ?"

"No, I am not a Christian," he replied. "But you have come at an opportune time. Perhaps you have heard that many of our men here are down with the plague; and every day, in spite of all that we can do, they are dying. I've just been sitting here wondering why these men have to die in the flower of their manhood. Perhaps you have the answers. Is it because they or their parents have sinned or because I have sinned or because our country has sinned? What does your Christian church say about it?"

The Chinese Pastor pulled the Bible from his bag and began to explain the way of salvation to the colonel. Inexplicably, he was impressed. Obviously the Lord had prepared his heart. That night they called together a few of the army officers to let them hear about the Christian way of life and to let them ask any questions that were on their hearts. This was repeated for three days — in the daytime talking to the colonel and, in the evening, meeting with the officers.

At the end of these talks the colonel was almost

convinced that Christianity is the true religion. He desperately wanted a Bible of his own so that he could study further to find the answers to his many questions. But during those war years Bibles were almost unavailable because they could not get across the firing lines to northwest China. Since the pastor had another Bible at home, he left his pocket edition with Joab and returned to his church. He reported to the members and the missionaries the hunger in the hearts of the army officers in that village and asked for prayer that something could be done to follow up his first exploratory trip.

I wanted to go with the pastor and help start services, but had other plans for the next week which I thought could not be changed easily. After teaching in the Northwest Bible Institute all week, early Saturday morning I hired a canopied horse cart to take me and our baby to a town twenty-five miles away to help a newly-opened church with its services.

Since neither cow's milk nor milk powder could be purchased in northwest China, I had to take a goat with me everywhere we went to provide milk for our youngest son. So that morning, first of all, the goat was lifted to the back of the canopied cart where she sat behind us on the floor and chewed her cud. Then we set the baby in his basket in the cart and the baggage beside him. I sat on the floor on one side of the front of the springless cart while the driver sat on the other side, except for the times that he walked or ran alongside the cart. There was no dashboard or other device to keep the horse's long tail from swishing mud from the road over the face and clothing of the passengers when the horse shooed off flies from his body.

The sun came out in all its glory that Saturday morning. Everyone looked for a weekend with clear skies. But the horsecart had not gone many miles down the road until black, ominous clouds overcast the sky and thunder rolled. When the rain began to pelt down, we pulled the front curtain down over the entrance of the cart and I sat inside with my feet folded under me, while the goat looked frightened because of the continuous thunder and the darkness under the canopy. A small piece of glass in the front curtain permitted the inside passengers to peep out and see what was going on. The driver tried to keep his clothes dry with an oiled poncho, as he ran alongside the horse.

The road would take us right through the village where Joab lived, but our plan was not to stop there that weekend. His village was situated in a valley between two steep mountains. As we descended the mountainside, the horse slid several times and almost sat down because of the slippery road. The cart was in danger of overturning.

"I can't take you any farther," the carter told me when we reached the village. "You saw how the horse slipped, trying to hold back the load. It is too dangerous for my beast. If I go on, I will have to climb that steep mountain road on the other side of the river, and I'm sure the road is too slippery. The horse won't be able to make it. Until the rain lets up I will not even be able to return home. We are stranded right here in this village for the present."

Was God changing my plans? Did He want me in this village over the weekend and had He sent the unexpected storm to prevent me from going farther?

"Please take me to Colonel Joab's house," I instructed the cart driver.

I had never met the colonel and didn't even know whether it would be convenient for me, the baby, and the goat to spend the weekend there. But, praying silently for guidance, I tapped on the gate of the courtyard. A young orderly opened it and seeing a

Western lady standing outside, quickly called Mrs. Joab to come. I was surprised that she seemed genuinely happy to see me.

"Pastor Wu has told me about you and about your husband's interest in Christianity," I began. "Will it be convenient for me and the baby to stay here with you over the weekend?"

"Come right in and put the baby on our brick bed. We have so many questions that we want to ask about Christianity. My husband and I have been taking turns reading the Bible that Pastor Wu left here, but there is so much we don't understand. I'm so glad you've come. Let me send to the office for my husband to come right home. He will certainly want to talk with you, too."

The goat was tethered in the yard by the time the colonel reached home.

"May we have a meeting of all the officers tonight and three times tomorrow?" he asked. "We are all trying to read the Bible, but we need someone to explain it to us. Major Mu's living room is larger than ours. Let me find out if we can have these four services in his home."

In a short time he made all the arrangements and also sent a messenger to inform all his officers of the meetings, urging them to attend.

At that time in northwest China, people sat on the brick bed on which the whole family slept. In the winter time this bed was heated from underneath by burning damp leaves, stalks, and dried manure. The colonel, his wife, and I sat on the bed while he plied me with questions about Christianity. By early afternoon the rain had stopped, and the sun shone again brightly. But it was now too late for me to continue my journey. Furthermore, it looked as though God had planned a weekend of meetings in this new village where two thousand troops were quartered and where the local people never had the gospel preached to them.

After an early supper, the officers and their wives gathered in the major's home. We could not sing because there were no hymnbooks. So as soon as all had arrived I began to tell them of the fall of man, God's plan of salvation, what God considers sin, and how to find Him. This took the whole evening.

That night, after the service, the colonel retired to his office where he slept on a cot, while I slept with his wife and family on the big brick bed. Or did we sleep? Mrs. Joab was in great distress of mind over her sins and kept asking if God could forgive her. She told me all of her terrible story just in case the missionary might be overestimating the love of God in saying she could be saved. She wanted to make sure that God could save a sinner whose sins were as great as hers.

Long after midnight when all the children were sound asleep, she knelt with me on the brick bed and, through her tears, for the first time in her life, poured out her heart to God. She told Him all about the sins of her past life and asked Him to forgive her. I wept silently beside her.

Suddenly she stopped praying and turning to me, she said, "I have peace in my heart. God has answered my prayer. I have never felt so peaceful in all my life. God has lifted the heavy burden from my heart. I am so happy! How can I thank Him enough?"

At daybreak we heard the colonel at the gate. The little orderly admitted him.

"Is Mrs. Taylor up yet?" he asked as he walked across the courtyard.

"Yes," the boy replied. "Up and dressed."

The colonel came walking into the room.

"Good morning!" he called out. "Do I look different? Just look at me. Do you see any difference?"

"What has happened?" I asked.

"I am a new person," he replied. "Last night after I went to my office I couldn't sleep. I took out my Bible and read it, but I couldn't keep my mind on what I was reading. I decided to kneel and pray. I didn't know how to pray, but from what you told us last night, I decided that I could at least confess my sins to God and ask Him to forgive me. Though I am a hardhearted man and never cry, the tears streamed down over my face as I told the Lord of my sins. It seemed that my heart was broken. I have been so wicked. Then I remembered that verse you had taught us, and I found it in my Bible, 'If we confess our sins He is faithful and just to forgive us our sins and to cleanse us from all unrighteousness.' It seemed that this was written just for me. I had confessed my sins. As I knelt there, I knew I was a new person. I knew that God had changed me. This morning everything looks different. I am sure that I've been changed. I used to hate my wife and children, but now my heart is overflowing with love for them. Come here, son!" He hugged his child until he squealed. "From now on your father will no longer kick you and be mean to you."

"Look at me," interrupted his wife. "I, too, am changed. Last night I knelt here on the bed and confessed my sins. I doubted that God could forgive such a sinner as I, but while I was praying, He came to my heart. I, too, am a new person. Our home life will be different from now on." She looked with loving eyes to her husband and he returned an affectionate look. It was not good Chinese custom for a man and his wife to embrace. But they certainly did it with their looks.

Sunday morning, afternoon, and evening at Major Mu's home, most of the same officers and their wives were present. They were all impressed by the change in Joab and his wife who gave their testimonies in the morning service. During the day both Major Mu and his wife sought and found the Lord in a public service, and at night the colonel of the second battalion also found God.

In the weeks that followed, regular services were held in this village. Both soldiers and civilians were invited. The local people were superstitious and idolatrous. They did not make changes easily. Since everyone in the village offered food and burned incense to the ancestors and to the idols, any who wanted to become Christians were afraid to do so lest they receive severe persecution from their neighbors. The work among local residents progressed slowly.

During the summer I took our baby and a milk goat so we could live in the village for two weeks and make a consecutive presentation of the gospel. A theatrical troupe came to the town at the same time as we and put on a puppet show in the temple courtyard every day. Village people and many from the surrounding country came in great crowds to see the two "shows."

After watching the puppet show at the temple, they came in large numbers to see the foreigner and her fairhaired baby. He was a great drawing card because all Chinese babies, in contrast, are born with black hair. They would run their fingers through his hair and then exclaim, "Imagine feeding a baby goat's milk. As a result he doesn't have *hair* on his head; he has goat's wool. He drinks goat's milk until he doesn't smell like a human being but like a goat." As soon as they had satisfied their curiosity about the baby, they would sit down, drink hot tea, and listen while our team of workers told them of Jesus and His love for mankind. Many posters were used to illustrate the gospel messages.

Joab's family and the other Christians among the military also helped in the evangelistic services.

Gradually superstition broke down, and some dared to take a public stand for Christ.

One difficulty we encountered in the work in the Northwest was that young married women were not permitted to go out on the streets unless they were accompanied by an elderly person. Usually the elders would escort them only once a year at the Chinese New Year season. One young woman, twenty-eight years of age, coming to our services when her elders came to see the theatrical performance and the baby, was converted. After that, since her elders would not come, she would slip into our little rented house through the back door because she had to come unnoticed through a narrow back lane, where no one would observe her. She enjoyed the services but knew that her elders in the home would not allow her on the street to attend. Turning to me one day she said, "Please pray for me that the Lord will soon make me forty years old so that I can go out on the streets alone. My mother-in-law is objecting to my coming, and I will have to do my worshiping of God at home."

"I am afraid that it will take God twelve years to answer that prayer," I replied.

Early one Sunday morning, months later, Joab appeared at our home. He looked troubled, and there was reason. Almost as soon as he sat down, he began to pour out his difficulty. He first told his distress to my husband and me and asked whether he might not tell it briefly to the congregation that morning and ask for their help in prayer. He had been drawing near to the Lord and asking Him to cleanse his heart and fill him with the Holy Spirit. As he had read the Word and prayed day after day, God revealed many things in his heart, one of which was the deception he used in the self-inflicted wound during the battle of Shanghai. God had made it clear that He would not allow dishonesty and deceit in the lives of His children.

Joab said, "I am now on my way to the provincial capital to see my commanding officer and there confess it all. I realize that he may execute me or at least imprison me. I have committed my wife and children into the Lord's care and am prepared to take the consequences. I can no longer conceal dishonesty in my life. God wants His children to be crystal clear before Him. Please pray that God's will may be done."

He arranged an appointment with his commanding officer at which time he poured out the whole story. The officer kept his scrutinizing eyes on him as he talked and, when he finished, asked, "Why did you tell me this? You know the penalty for such a crime. No one knew about it. Why are you uncovering it now?"

"I am telling you," he replied, "because some months ago I became a Christian, and Christians must not allow any deceit in the heart. I realize the penalty and am prepared for you to punish me as you think the crime deserves. I have not come to plead for mercy."

The commanding officer sat in deep thought for some minutes and then replied, "This is the first time that I have ever encountered this kind of situation. And you say you have come to confess it because you have become a Christian. Go back home and wait there until I think it over and decide how to handle your case. Don't return until I send for you."

As soon as Joab left the headquarters, his commander called for one of his officers and said, "Go throughout this city and search for a Chinese pastor of some intelligence and ask him to come here. I want him to tell me what Christianity is all about."

The officer went and finally returned with a Chinese pastor who sat there for several hours answering questions and explaining the teachings of Christ to him. Some of the Christians had been praying for a long time that God would save this commanding officer. Now God was using the confession of Joab to show the power of Christ's gospel. Some years later both the commander and his wife became earnest Christians.

Until his punishment should be decided, Joab was relieved of all responsibilities. Remaining at home, he spent much time reading his Bible and praying daily. After nearly six weeks, he received a letter from his commanding officer ordering him to appear at headquarters. He went with apprehension, not knowing what disposition might be made of his case.

When he was ushered into the room, his superior said gruffly, "I should, according to justice, let you go before the firing squad. But since you have had courage enough to confess your crime, I have decided that I would be foolish to execute a man who has become thoroughly honest and trustworthy. I need your kind of officer in my troops. So instead of executing you, I am offering you a position as commandant of an officer's training school. There are a lot of rough young men in this school whom no one has been able to control. I want you to take them over and see what you can do with them."

Joab asked for several days to think and pray about it. Days later he replied, "I will take over this school on one condition — that you will allow me to have Chinese preachers and missionaries come to the school and hold regular services for the cadets. It is only the salvation of Jesus Christ that will change their hearts."

The officer replied, "I am turning them over to you. Use what methods you think best. I now promote you to brigadier general while you are commandant of this school. Good luck to you."

Brigadier General Joab walked out of headquarters with his head high. Not only had God forgiven him, but now he could look every man in the face and know that there were no hidden sins lurking in his heart. He returned home to help move his family to the site of the school. Now his children no longer feared him when he came home. His little boy and the girls would run to the gate to meet their father and feel into his pockets for hard candy or peanuts that they knew he always kept for them. He was, indeed, a new person.

After selecting a new staff and reorganizing the school, he set the day for the opening. He asked my husband, and a Chinese colleague, Mark, to conduct chapel services every morning following early drill and again each evening. He required the students to fall into military formation and file into the building for church services. Many of the students were definitely not interested in compulsory religious services. But if they attended this school under the new administration, they must conform to the rules. Some slumped down in their seats and pretended not to be listening. But it was clear that they were absorbing a lot that was being said. Both of the speakers preached on sin and God's remedy for it. Most of the students had never before heard a gospel sermon. They were surprised to hear these two preachers, one a Westerner and the other a Chinese, speak so frankly about sin — yes, the sins that they were committing every day. The truth spoke to many hearts.

At the close of each service, an invitation was given for those who wanted to seek the Lord to come forward and pray. Many responded; and after Christ had come into their hearts, they would witness to the others of the change Christ had made in them.

Some confessed to having murdered those who opposed them. Others told of going out at night to remove the telephone wire along the roads in the area and then sell it for cash. Still others told of stealing and eating chickens owned by the farmers of the area. One time when the commanding officer was visiting the school, he remarked to the principal after he listened to some of the testimonies, "Man, you are not dealing with men here at this school; you are dealing with tigers!"

Not all of the students were willing to forsake their way of life and become Christians. Some opposed the preaching. One man wrote a discourteous, anonymous letter to the preachers and said that if they did not get out of there in a hurry, they would be killed. That night my husband announced publicly that he had received an anonymous letter warning them that if Mark and he did not leave, their lives would be in danger. He added, "You are soldiers of the Republic of China. In your position as soldiers fighting the enemy of your country, if you received a letter from the enemy threatening that if you did not flee you would be killed, would you run away?"

A loud "No" resounded from all parts of the auditorium.

"In like manner," replied Mr. Taylor, "we are soldiers of the King of Kings. We do not intend to run away. We plan to remain right here at our post until our work is finished." And stay they did.

Many of the students were converted and their exemplary lives became a rebuke to the others who wanted to continue living in sin. Gradually the whole moral standard of the academy was raised until those who wanted to commit wicked deeds were deterred by their classmates.

Joab remained in charge of the academy until the close of World War II. Soon after the war ended, feeling that there was no longer the urgent need of his services in the military, he asked to be relieved of his post and returned to civilian life. He sensed that the greatest need of China was the spreading of the gospel of Jesus Christ which he knew so well from personal experience is able to make a basic transformation in the life from within. God was leading him to devote full time to the work of spreading the gospel. From place to place he went telling what great things God had done in his life. He led many to turn to Christ.

Chapter Six

JAMES

THE GOD OF WEALTH

"Let me help you tie that," called Mark to me. He finished tying the roll of bedding tightly on the back carrier of my bicycle using his own rope. On the sixteen-mile ride to the railroad station it would be important not to have to stop and pick up a roll of bedding. We wouldn't dare lose it during the cold weather. No family would have extra bedding for guests during the winter.

"Thank you for giving that last strong pull," I replied. "I never was good at tying bundles on a bicycle. I am glad that I got my bedding washed and clean for this trip. Did your wife get your quilts taken apart, washed, and put back together again?"

"Yes," he said. "She just finished my quilt yesterday. We have both been so busy cleaning house and getting ready for the New Year that we haven't had time for anything else." Then, he told how on the last sunny day everyone moved all the furniture out of doors, scrubbed it, and moved it back into a clean house. His wife had made new clothes for each member of the family and also new shoes. She was busy for two months.

We swung the straw baskets containing our Bibles, hymnbooks, and tracts over the handlebars of the bicycles and were on our way to the railroad station sixteen miles away. Our clothing was wrapped inside the rolls of bedding.

"Everyone else is too busy to take time to listen to preaching these days," said Mark. "It is a good thing that the military people don't pay much attention to celebrating New Year. Otherwise we could not have any meetings this week."

"We will have to stop in the city and buy some boxes of sweets and some fruit to give to our host and hostess," I called to remind him. All the people along the roads going home were carrying brightly-wrapped packages of sweets and fruit. The old saying was literally being carried out, "No one comes home at Chinese New Year with an empty hand."

"Since they will be entertaining us for these few days, we will have to buy something really good," he advised.

Perspiring profusely after our long ride, we left our bicycles with a friend near the depot. Then carrying our rolls of bedding on our shoulders, we started for the train station. The ubiquitous roll of bedding is an essential part of every traveler's equipment in the cold weather.

"The train will be crowded beyond capacity," said Mark. "Look at the crowd of people already standing on the platform waiting for the train. I will see if I can buy the tickets for both of us. I hope they are still selling them."

He soon returned with two tickets and we joined the throng of people milling about on the platform. There were already enough people standing there to fill a train completely, and this was the third station from the starting point.

"Let me tie those two rolls of bedding together," said Mark. "You carry the two packages of Bibles and I'll handle the bedding rolls."

As the train whistled its approach, we could see that already there were passengers sitting on the top of the coaches, clinging to any part of the engine where they could get a grip, or hanging onto the brass handles at the entrance of each coach. Where would we be able to squeeze on?

"Is it presumptuous of us to expect God to help us find a little spot on this crowded train?" I asked Mark. "It is already more than filled."

"Jump down off the platform quickly," said Mark as he hopped down onto the tracks. "Let us try for a place on the side of the train opposite the platform. We stand a better chance over there."

We had just found a stance when the engine swept past us with the overloaded coaches following. As the coaches passed us, we watched frantically for a little place where we might crowd on.

"Come on up here, Mrs. Taylor and Pastor Mark," a voice called out as the first class coach swept past us. "Come here and sit with us. There is plenty of room. Give us your baggage."

We looked up to see the familiar face of Colonel Su. He and his wife and children, bound for the provincial capital to spend the New Year, were seated in a private compartment along with a military friend of theirs, Chief of Staff James, with his pretty concubine and his eight-year-old son. Quickly we squeezed through the jostling crowd and scrambled up the steps. When we and our baggage got into that compartment, it was crowded. But as compared with the rest of the train, we had ample room. The military attendants sat on rolls of bedding in the passageway while we enjoyed a seat in the compartment.

"Meet my friend, Chief of Staff James," said Colonel Su. We arose, bowed, and shook hands.

When the conductor came by, we gladly made up the difference between our third class tickets and the unexpected provision of this first class compartment.

"Mrs. Taylor, will you please tell the chief of staff

about Jesus?" asked the colonel when the conductor left. "We are returning from a meeting of people from my province where I have been trying to tell them how good it is to be a Christian. Some have listened to me, but this man has repulsed my every effort and refuses to listen further to anything that deals with religion."

Such an introduction gave little inspiration or hope that we might accomplish much with this officer. I prayed silently and then began. The chief of staff listened very attentively at first as I told him about the fall of man, of God's plan of salvation for the whole world, and of God's yearning to redeem sinners. He listened intently because he had never before heard a foreigner talk in his language and a foreign woman, at that! It fascinated him at first. But when the truth began to strike home, and I began to talk about God's power to save sinners, he interrupted.

"That's a very good dissertation, and thought-provoking, but it doesn't apply to me. You see, I am a 'moral prince,' therefore, I do not need this salvation. I am not a sinner. The only god that can interest me at present is the god of wealth. Can you tell me about him? With my aged parents, my wife, and children, and this concubine to support, my salary is insufficient. I am interested in money, not in a religion about sinners being changed."

"But we are telling you about the God of wealth," I replied. "The Bible says 'For every animal of the forest is mine, and the cattle on a thousand hills' (Psalm 50:10). 'The silver is mine, and the gold is mine, declares the Lord Almighty' (Haggai 2:8)."

He was suddenly all attention again.

But I was puzzled. How should I proceed? How could I convince a high army officer who declared that he is a "moral prince" that he is a sinner in need of Christ's forgiveness? Then I remembered Romans

3:20 "Through the law we become conscious of sin," and Galatians 3:24 "The law was put in charge to lead us to Christ, that we might be justified by faith."

Then, with a smile, I continued. "Mr. James, as I look at you, I can see that you have not gone into a lot of the wickedness that has overtaken many other men. As man looks at you, he would call you a "moral prince." But God does not look upon sin as man does. In China you say that murder, arson, and perhaps adultery are sins. But let us see what God says. He includes more in sin than man does. Since He will be our final judge, let us see what His Word says!"

We put a Bible into his hand and turned to the twentieth chapter of Exodus, which records the Ten Commandments.

"Now, Sir, we want you to see what God calls sin. Will you count how many of God's commandments you have violated? Let us read the first commandment. 'You shall have no other gods before me.' Have you ever worshiped God?"

"No," he replied. "I have never heard of Him until recently. How could I worship Him? I will have to plead guilty to breaking that one."

"Let us look at the second commandment, 'You shall not make for yourself an idol in any form . . . You shall not bow down to them, or worship them.' Have you ever worshiped idols?" I continued.

"Yes," he answered, "I have. I really don't believe in them; but when I was a boy, because my parents wanted me to worship the idols, I complied. Even now, I worship idols to please them. So I suppose I have violated that commandment, too."

"Number three." I let him read, "You shall not misuse the name of the Lord your God." "Do you ever use the name of the Reverend Heavenly Grandfather (a common name for God in China) carelessly in exclamations or in complaining of His doings?"

"Yes," he responded. "Those are common practices of mine. I never thought of that as a sin, but I suppose it is not reverent. So I am guilty of violating the third commandment, also."

I went on. "Look at number four, 'Remember the Sabbath day by keeping it holy.' Do you use this day as a time of rest and of worship of the true God?"

"Of course not," he said. "Sunday is my busiest day. It is usually on that day that I call the staff meetings or I go traveling to see my friends. That is my most strenuous day of the week. Again, I will have to admit guilt."

"Let's look at the fifth commandment," I said. " 'Honor your father and your mother.' Have you done this?"

Happily, he replied, "You don't get me on this one. I am a filial son. No one can say that I do not respect and support my parents."

"But," I said, "when you were young, did you disobey them, cause them grief, irritate them? Did you cause them anxiety in your younger days because of your willful ways?"

"I fear I must plead guilty," he replied, "if you are going to include what happened when I was younger. I was willful and demanded my own way. This caused my parents many a heartache. Yes, I am guilty."

"What does the next one say?" I asked. " 'You shall not murder.' "

"How can I be a soldier and not kill?" he asked. "I have killed many of the enemy. Can a Christian not fight for his country?"

"God is not talking of national enemies here," I replied. "The Bible records many wars that were waged where God commanded His children to fight and helped them to win. Even Christ said, 'My kingdom is not of this world. If my kingdom were of this world, then would my servants fight.' In the fifth commandment He is talking about the murder of our personal enemies. Have you killed any of them? Or have you hated any of them? The Bible says, 'Anyone who hates his brother is a murderer.' Have you ever hated anyone?"

"Yes," he replied, "I have not only hated people, but I have killed three personal enemies and have two more that I plan to kill when I have the opportunity. So if hating is the same as killing, then I am guilty of violating this commandment also."

"Let us look at the seventh commandment," I continued, pointing to the Bible. "Read that, please."

" 'You shall not commit adultery,' " he read. "Everyone commits that sin. We Chinese look upon this as a physical necessity. When a man is away from his wife, he needs sexual comfort. Of course, I have committed that sin, if you call it a sin." Sitting beside him was his highly-painted, play-doll concubine who traveled with him when he was away from home.

"What does God say is the next sin?" I asked. "Please note the eighth commandment, 'You shall not steal.' "

His face lit up. "I come from a wealthy home. If we wanted pears to eat, we went to our own orchard and picked them. If we wanted melons to eat, we had our own melon patch and could eat all we wanted. I have never stolen. On this point. I am not guilty."

How was this "moral prince" to see that he had committed the sin of stealing? "Mr. James," I said, "you are an official in the Chinese army. Have you ever padded your rosters in order to collect additional money and grain? Because the salaries set by the government are low, have you ever reported more men in your division than there actually were, and then collected their salaries and grain and divided what you received with the other officers?"

Seriously he replied, "If you are talking about that, there are few officers in the whole military organization who do not pad the rosters. Of course, I have done it. How could I make a decent living for myself and my family if I didn't? If that is a sin, then I have broken that commandment also."

" 'You shall not give false testimony,' " we read on. "Have you ever told lies?"

"Who hasn't?" he replied. "I wouldn't give a dime for a man who doesn't lie. Look at my son sitting there. He is so naive. He doesn't have intelligence to tell a lie. When someone comes to my home to see me and presents his card to a servant or to my son to give to me, if it is someone that I do not care to see, I simply say, 'Tell him that I am not at home.' My silly son goes out and says to the caller, 'My father says he isn't at home.' What will such an honest son amount to when he grows up? Of course, I have lied."

"Look at the last commandment, 'You shall not covet,' " I read. "Do you covet? Do you look upon other people's houses, wives, servants, or money and wish they were yours?"

A thoughtful Mr. James replied, "Of course I covet. I am not satisfied with what I get and covet that which belongs to others. Did I not tell you that at present I am interested only in worshiping the god of wealth? I crave money so that I can live lavishly."

By this time the chief of staff was serious. He sat there in deep thought as he glanced again at the Ten Commandments. The compartment was quiet as he made an evaluation of his past life and compared his standard of morals with that of the Bible.

Finally he broke the silence by saying, "By these standards I am not a moral prince. I am a sinner. I have never thought of sin in this light before. I am a sinner. What can I do about it?"

"At the beginning of our trip we told you how God loves sinners and sent His Son, Jesus, into this world to die for us sinners," I said. "He is waiting not only to forgive your sins but also to put new life within you, which will give you power to overcome sin. Look, here in I John 1:9 is the plan that God gives us. 'If we confess our sins, he is faithful and just and will forgive us our sins, and purify us from all unrighteousness.' If you will tell God about your past sins and failures, He will forgive you and make you a new person. He has done it for all of us who are sitting here with you, and He can do it for you."

I paused, wondering whether to pray with the chief of staff on the train. "What is your destination, Mr. James?" I asked.

He answered, "'I am going to see a friend who lives in Three Bridges. I plan to spend a few days at his home."

Three Bridges was the town in which our week of meetings was scheduled.

"The Lord has arranged it so that you may find Him," I told him. "Pastor Mark will preach there at seven o'clock tonight in the home of Colonel Joab. Plan to come."

"I'll be there," he replied.

That night Mr. James, his son, and his concubine appeared at the service along with many other military personnel. We all crowded into Joab's living room and sat on small wooden benches that had been borrowed for the meetings. God helped Pastor Mark give a masterful presentation of the plan of salvation. As he closed, he asked, "Who among us feels the need of this new life which God alone can give? Stand up right where you are and pray for God to forgive you."

Without hesitation Mr. James arose, and with his eyes wide open, (no one had thought to tell him that Christians close their eyes when they pray), he fixed his eyes on a red paper cross that Colonel Joab had pasted on the wall of his living room to indicate to all who entered his home that he is a Christian. Mr. James told the Lord all about the meeting on the train with the Christians and how he had said that he did not need this foreign religion because he looked upon himself as a moral prince but that they had shown him from the Bible that he was a sinner. With the marvelous accuracy of a Chinese memory, he went down the line of the Ten Commandments in perfect order and told the Lord that he was guilty of violating each one.

He closed his prayer by saying, "O God, I am that sinner for whom Jesus died. I am not a moral prince. Can you save me from my sins and make me a new person?"

Just then he turned his gaze to the others who were sitting on their stools in the room and called out with ecstatic joy, "Oh! He's done it! He has come to my heart. He has given me this new life."

At the beginning of the service we had taught the congregation to sing the hymn:

All my life long I had panted
  For a draught from some cool spring
That I hoped would quench the burning
  Of the thirst I felt within.

Feeding on the husks around me,
  Till my strength was almost gone;
Longed my soul for something better,
  Only still to hunger on.

Poor I was and sought for riches,
  Something that would satisfy,
But the dust I gathered round me
  Only mocked my soul's sad cry.

Well of water, ever springing,
    Bread of life, so rich and free,
Untold wealth that never faileth,
    My Redeemer is to me.

CHORUS:
Hallelujah! I have found Him
    Whom my soul so long has craved!
Jesus satisfies my longings;
    Through His blood I now am saved.

The whole group broke into singing this song as soon as Mr. James had found God. Then others in the room arose and prayed. For three days the services continued with many seeking and finding the Lord.

The afternoon of the third day Mr. James came to us and said, "I want to return to the city from which I have just come. When I was there a week ago and Colonel Su tried to tell us about Jesus, I ridiculed him and his religion and would have nothing to do with it. Now I want to return, call these friends together again and tell them that I am a Christian and pass on to them all that I have heard here these days. Will you please pray for me as I go back that God will use my testimony to tell them so clearly that they will understand and want to believe in Jesus? I can sing that hymn we learned all the way through. Listen to me as I sing and see if I sing it right." Though he sang off key, the words came from an overflowing heart. "Untold wealth that never faileth, my Redeemer is to me."

He carried a precious new Bible with him and went on his way. Later he told us that one couple was saved through his testimony to the change God had made in his life.

He was transferred to a place where he was in charge of a military grain depot where tons of wheat were stored. He wrote to us that truly he had found the God of Wealth. On his official stationery he had printed the hymn that he had learned at the meeting in Colonel Joab's home. He began to hold services for his officers and men in his own home and asked some of us to come and help him lead the people who attended to the Lord. He was longing for the day when the war would be over and he could be free to attend Bible school and learn how to be an effective instrument in the hands of God! He had truly become not only an officer in the army of China, but also an officer in the army of the Lord. He kept busy finding new recruits for God.

When I visited China in 1980 you can imagine my joy when Brother James came to see me. After all these years he could still sing from memory the song he had learned the day he was born again.

Chapter Seven

SUE

THE EVANGELIST'S DAUGHTER

"A little happiness is born to you this time," the midwife whispered to Pastor Ding, a well-known evangelist in North China on the occasion of the birth of his third child.

"Thank you, Lord!" he exclaimed. "She shall have every opportunity that a son would have. We will show the heathen world that we Christians are grateful to God for all that He gives us. She shall have as good an education as boys get even though few parents are educating their girls. Why deny a girl schooling because her education will benefit her husband's rather than her parents' home? Yes, my 'Little Happiness' shall lead the way in showing what a girl can do."

From the day of her birth Pastor Ding had a special love for Sue. Whenever he returned from his long evangelistic tours, he delighted in carrying her out on the streets for the neighbors to see. Most of the other fathers were carrying boys and were proud to display the ones who would later bring a bride to the home and raise up offspring who would carry on the family name and inherit the family property.

When Sue was less than three years old, Pastor Ding was thrilled to find that she could carry a tune accurately. He took delight in teaching her Christian choruses and hymns. With her high, clear voice she

99

entertained the neighbors with her songs.

Inwardly Pastor Ding planned, "She shall have the best education I can give her. I want her to receive special training in both vocal and instrumental music so that she can accompany me on my evangelistic tours. Her music will add much to the interest and the success of the meetings. Yes, my little Sue shall have the best."

She joined with the neighbors' boys in attending classes conducted by a private teacher who was employed by the parents of the pupils. She kept right up with the boys in learning the Chinese classics and mathematics. When she finished the elementary classes, she would have to find a girls' school that she could attend; for in those days, as soon as girls and boys reached adolescence, they attended separate schools. Because normally the girls lived behind the high walls of their courtyards and never went out on the streets except at the time of Chinese New Year when they were accompanied by senior women of the home, most towns had no schools for girls. If they went to high school, they must find a boarding school, usually operated by missionaries.

Sue was sent to a well-known girls' school in Shanghai which was patronized by daughters of wealthy families. Her father would escort her to the school in the fall and get her at the close of the term the following summer. Sue found it difficult to observe strict economy when her classmates, girls from affluent homes, could spend almost limitless amounts of money. Her parents were sacrificing to send her there and could make little provision for spending money. By the time they paid for her board, room, travel, and books, they and the rest of the family had to economize in order to make ends meet.

One day when her classmates were spending money lavishly, Sue had a severe temptation to practice dishonesty. One wealthy girl always had money to spend. Sue seldom had any. She became bold enough to ask her classmate to lend her a dollar, which, for her, was a large sum of money. She had no intention of repaying the loan, nor did she do so. Her friend had so much to spend that she never asked Sue to repay it. So Sue dismissed the matter from her mind. She felt that she had been clever in getting some spending money.

High school days flew past rapidly; the time of graduation was fast approaching. What would Sue do when she finished high school? She could have found many positions open to her in the big cities. But her father felt that both her vocal and instrumental musical talent should be developed further in order that she might be of the greatest usefulness in spreading the gospel. He was able to procure a scholarship for her to a famous college for women in America where she would receive the best training by renowned professors.

Pastor Ding's heart rejoiced as he and a missionary friend saw her off on a ship to America. They both urged her to apply herself to her lessons and get the most out of her courses, and then return to China to help in building up the Christian church. Their enthusiasm was so infectious that as Sue waved her farewells to them from the deck of the ship, her heart swelled with pride as she thought how highly honored she was to have been chosen from millions of girls to take further training in America. She would get all the best pointers she could from her American professors and come back to use them for the uplifting of her fellow-countrymen. The anticipation of it all so thrilled her that she found little time for homesickness.

After Sue entered college, she read her Bible daily and also took time for morning and evening private devotions. But she soon came to realize that few of her classmates had time or interest for private Bible study and prayer. For a time she was almost overwhelmed. She reasoned within herself, "Is this not Christian America? Why do these young people not take their faith in Christ more seriously?"

She received a second jolt when her science professor seemed to take delight in criticizing the Bible and in speaking slurringly of its "inaccuracies." In fact, one day he went so far as to say, "The Bible is an obsolete book, not at all relevant to our modern age. Time spent in reading the Bible is wasted. Few modern students read it."

Because Sue wanted to be modern and not different from her classmates, she took her Bible and buried it in the bottom of her trunk. When she returned to China, she would convince her father that modern Christians no longer spend time on Bible reading and prayer. She desired to be like the others. Were they not all Christians? Gradually her attendance at church services also decreased. Her Sundays were spent in sightseeing or in preparing her lessons for the next day.

Upon completion of her course at the Christian college, Sue received a scholarship for graduate study in the science department of Columbia University. At that time students from China and especially girl students were so few that it was not too difficult to obtain a scholarship to the larger universities. The institutions of higher learning felt that by training promising young people they were training future leaders of these emerging countries and were thereby giving valuable assistance to these nations.

Sue threw all her energies into her graduate studies in biological science. She thought of the high salary that she would command as a teacher when she returned to China. She also looked forward with anticipation to a prosperous domestic life in her homeland. Since so few Chinese girls had gone abroad for the completion of their education, she was now in the category of girls in great demand as wives of wealthy officials or businessmen. She was an apt student and an earnest follower of the customs and ways of the most advanced nation in the world. Her hair-do, clothing, eating habits, and way of life were now thoroughly American, and she wanted to transplant this culture to her native country.

Days flew by quickly, and the time came for her to return to China. As she packed her trunks to return home, it began to dawn on her with overwhelming force that she was now having to leave the new culture and to return to the culture of her childhood. Conditions would have changed very little. Only in the big cities like Shanghai and Peking, where many Westerners had come to carry on their business, would there be much change. How and where could she fit in?

She was also perplexed with the question of how she would break the news to her father that she had no intention of accompanying him on his evangelistic tours. She already anticipated how brokenhearted he would be. As a daughter into whose heart from earliest childhood had been deeply instilled the Confucian law of filial piety, this was the last thing she should do. For days Sue pondered the subject.

She was reluctant to wreck her future life by complying with her father's wishes. He belonged to the old culture. She was returning to her homeland with high hopes and ideas of promoting the new Western culture.

Following days and weeks of mental unrest and perturbation, she came to her decision. She would break the news to her father as soon as she met him when she disembarked from the ship in Shanghai. She would be straightforward and frank as they were in

America. She would ask him to return to his work without her, while she would find suitable work in Shanghai where Western culture had already taken a foothold.

As the ship sailed slowly up the Woosung River to the docks in Shanghai, she could see in the distance her father and the same missionary friend who had seen her off to America, standing on the dock and waving with their handkerchiefs the heartiest of welcomes to the young traveler from abroad. Her heart beat fast as she thought how deep the hurt would be that she would soon inflict on her loving father. But she remained resolute and planned how she would break the news quickly. As the ship pulled up to the dock, she was one of the first of the passengers to run down the gangplank to shake hands with those awaiting her on the pier.

Pastor Ding grasped one hand and the missionary the other as they both tried to speak their welcomes at the same time. Chinese custom forbade their embracing or kissing.

Then her father addressed her and said, "Sue, you do not know how I have been looking forward to this day! When you were a child I dedicated you to the Lord. I saw to it that you received the best training possible for the Lord's work. I can hardly believe that you are really back home and ready to travel with me in His work. I have many engagements for both of us for this summer and fall. Right now we have a heavy schedule of conferences and conventions planned for the summer. You can play the organ or piano and assist with the vocal music as well as do personal work between services. You don't know my joy at seeing you back in your own homeland. Let me help get your baggage through customs."

Sue's heart beat even more rapidly as she replied, "Father, it is so good to be back with you again. I was thrilled to see you and our dear missionary friend on the dock to meet me. I have been away a long time. And as you say, I have had opportunity to acquire a good education at some of the best schools. But now I need to go into the city immediately and find a teaching position where I can earn money to help the family finances."

"But, Sue," her father interrupted, "God will take care of the family finances. China needs you and your talents in the evangelistic field. You are already announced and we must proceed at once into the summer schedule of meetings. I need you. God needs you."

"Father," Sue began, "I hate to grieve you. I no longer believe as I did before I went to America. Most of the Christians I knew there did not read their Bibles, and our professors told us that many things recorded in the Bible are untrue and unscientific. I plan to find a position and earn money. After all, I must plan my own life."

Her bluntness and tactlessness were certainly of the Western culture. No Chinese would ever deal in such a cruel manner with a loving parent. Her father was stunned. So was the missionary. It seemed that her father groped to find something to cling to for support. He and the missionary, deeply wounded, looked alternately from each other to Sue. Had they heard correctly? Was this, indeed, the young woman for whom they had made sacrifices to educate? Could she show such base ingratitude and reply so cruelly after all they had done for her? For a time they were too stunned to speak.

Sue finally broke the silence by saying, "I must see my baggage through customs and then find a place to stay while I look for work."

Her father, with drooping shoulders and bowed head, walked with her to the customs building at the end of the pier. His grief of heart was too deep for words. He only wished that he could find a quiet place where he could withdraw from the crowds and weep out his heart before the Lord.

A few days later found Pastor Ding alone on the train en route to his meetings, and Sue settled in her newly-rented apartment in Shanghai. A feeling of remorse nagged at her heart as she recalled the crushed spirit of her father as he bade her good-bye. But she said aloud to herself, "After all, it is my life to plan."

It was not difficult for Sue to find a position teaching in a high school with a good salary. With people of high social standing and affluence as her intimate friends, she threw herself into the high life of the cosmopolitan port city of Shanghai. She was far too busy with her social activities to find time to attend church services.

In her rounds of pleasure she met many promising young men who were looking for a life companion who could take her places in the social life of the big cities. Most of the young women, even those from wealthy homes, were illiterate and had bound feet. Footbinding had now been prohibited by the government. In a few years wives who had bound feet would be taboo in society. Sue with her fine education and natural feet was very popular with the young men.

The man who impressed her most was Ernest, a widower with four children, who had attended Harvard University in America. He was extremely alert mentally and gave promise of a successful career in the government. The one drawback was that he was a Buddhist who knew little or nothing of Christianity. Since his ancestors were idolators, he followed in their footsteps. He attended church a few times when he was at Harvard, but saw nothing different in the lives of church members from his own, nor was there anything attractive about their religion. No Christians in America had thought to invite him to come to their homes while they explained the meaning of Christianity to him. So, why change? He had been a Buddhist when he went to America and was still one when he returned.

Sue felt sure that her parents would object to her marrying a Buddhist. In past years parents chose the life partners for their children and made the plans for their weddings. Modern Chinese young people were beginning to break away from the old custom and were choosing their own spouses, though usually after conferring with their parents.

Again Sue flouted her parents' wishes and made her own choice of a life companion. She informed them that she was engaged to Ernest, a young Buddhist, who was a widower with four children. He had been educated in America and now had a good position in a government agency. She invited them to attend the wedding. With a sad and heavy heart her father attended the ceremony. He wanted Sue to know that he loved her and was interested in everything that concerned her. But, daily he prayed that God would by some means restore her faith.

Shortly after Sue's wedding her husband was transferred to another post in an eastern city where she became a popular socialite. Chinese pastors and missionaries out of deference to her father called in her home, but she never found it convenient to attend church services. She and her husband rented a home with a large garden which had a lotus pond near the house. They had servants to do all the work in the home which gave Sue plenty of time to practice on the piano and keep up her vocal exercises. She had a rich, mellow, soprano voice and played her own graceful accompaniment on the piano. Her husband's four children loved to hear her sing.

Sue was not too excited that her first child was a girl, but her joy knew no bounds when, over a year later, a bouncing boy was born. She asked her own father to choose a name for him. He named the baby David and visited their home to participate in the customary feast when the first son was a month old. It seemed that he had never seen a more attractive child. Whenever he was in that area he spent a few days visiting Sue and playing with his grandchildren. Sue was very proud of her happy little boy.

One afternoon as Sue was playing the piano, David, who was then nearly three years old, came into the drawing room and began to coax her to give him something. She replied, "Run outside and play. Mother is busy." And away he ran.

In a few minutes he was back again coaxing and again she sent him away. When he came the third time, she became impatient with him because he persisted in disturbing her. Arising from the piano bench, she charged angrily at him, saying, "Go away from me and find something to do outside! I want to finish practicing this music. Then I'll get you what you want. Now go away and don't come back."

Frightened at his mother's anger, David ran outside.

Shortly afterward Sue regretted her severity with her son and decided to hunt him up and comfort him. She reasoned, "I should not have been so severe with him. He does not realize that I like to hold myself to a strict daily practicing schedule. I will go now and comfort him."

She went out into the garden to look for him, but saw no sign of him anywhere. Then she called, "David! David!" There was no reply. She ordered the servants to go out on the street in front of their yard to see if he had gone there. But they could find him nowhere. She was now becoming desperate.

"Could he have gone to the lotus pond to play?" she asked. She and the servants ran together to the lotus pond. Sue let out a scream as she saw that David had lost his balance and had drowned in the pond. After they had recovered his body, they tried artificial respiration and called for a doctor. But it was too late. Precious little David was dead! She sent for her husband, who was away from home, and also sent a wire for her father to come. Chinese Christians and missionaries hearing of the tragedy, came and offered comfort and any services they could give.

One missionary comforted the grieving parents with the following illustration: "When the shepherd wants to get the mother sheep to go into better pastures, he picks up her lamb in his arms and carries it there. The mother will follow. In like manner sometimes when God cannot get the attention of the parent, he picks up one of the little ones in His arms and carries it to heaven. If you will follow Him, eventually you will be with your precious David again."

Sue's father stayed with Ernest and Sue several days, trying to comfort them and win their hearts to the Lord. Ernest decided that he would become a Christian. He immediately began to read a Bible, which his father-in-law had given him, and to pray. He received the assurance that God had come to his heart. From this time forward he would follow the Lord.

But for Sue, the road was not so easy. She had lost her faith. She had listened to godless professors in America and had believed them rather than the Bible. Now, though she tried to believe in God, when she attempted to pray it was as though a voice said, "The Bible is obsolete. It is not relevant to our modern times. Its teachings are not dependable. Time spent in reading it is wasted." She tried hard to believe, but faith did not come.

It was at this juncture that the family was moved to a neighboring provincial capital where Ernest was placed in charge of the tax bureau controlling the whole province. God timed the move just right. Sue's father, Pastor Ding, was at that time conducting a week of evangelistic services in our church in that city. Ernest came every evening and ate supper in our home with his father-in-law and then remained for the evening meeting. His faith and knowledge of the Christian way were deepened during those days.

Sue, who arrived two weeks later than her husband, missed the meetings completely. The day after her arrival she visited our home where she poured out to us the sad story of her loss of faith and of the death of her son. She concluded, "Now, try as I will, I cannot get my faith back. My husband is so happy in his newfound faith, but I am so hopeless. I have prayed and prayed, but there is no answer." Together we prayed, but still there was no answer.

"I must return home," she said after some time of futile praying. "Our new baby must be fed. I must go at once."

"Before you retire tonight," I suggested, "pray this prayer, 'Holy Spirit, search my heart and show me what keeps me from finding peace with God.' He is faithful and will make it clear."

The next afternoon she came again to our home. "I don't know why I can't find peace," she said sadly as she came in the door.

"Did you pray the prayer I suggested?" I asked. "What did God show you?"

"There are two things that keep coming to my mind, but I don't think they should make any difference," she replied. "When I was in America getting ready to leave the Christian college and enter Columbia University, all of us girls brought our trunks and suitcases into one room and visited as we packed up before separating. Our things were all spread out on the tables and beds as we sorted and packed them. Suddenly I saw an unusual pair of scissors lying there on a table. I had never seen a pair like them and wanted them so much. When no one was looking I took them and packed them in my trunk and I still have them. What can I do about them now?"

"Do you know which girl they belonged to?" I asked.

"No," she replied. "We all had our things spread out in one room and I did not know at the time to whom they belonged. I have no way of writing to the school for an address because I don't know whose they were."

"In that case," I replied, "estimate their value and give the money for some needy cause. Then the devil cannot taunt you about having someone else's goods in your home."

She reached in her purse and brought out many times the value of the scissors, saying as she did so, "Here, take this, and use it to buy tracts for evangelism. I will certainly be glad to get that load off my heart. Every time I have seen those scissors I have felt so dishonest."

"What is your second problem?" I asked.

"It seems such a senseless thing, but I cannot get it off my mind," she replied. "Some weeks ago, I went into a dress goods store to buy cloth for the family. I chose three pieces that I wanted and gave them to a clerk to figure on the abacus the amount I owed and then to wrap them up for me. In my own mind I had figured the amount of my bill and had taken enough money from my purse to pay it. But as the clerk figured the bill, he failed to see one piece of cloth and did not charge me for it. He asked me four dollars less than my bill should have been. I removed the four dollars from the bills in my hand and returned them to my purse. In my heart I reasoned, 'If a shop employs clerks that cannot figure accounts, that is their fault. I was prepared to pay my complete bill, but he didn't ask for it. The fault is his, not mine. I shouldn't be held responsible for it.' "

"Who brought this matter to your mind?" I asked. "I did not because I knew nothing about it."

She replied, "I suppose God did it. But what face have I to go back to the store and confess it? My husband holds an important position in this city. If I confess my dishonesty, it will injure his reputation."

"Do you want peace with God?" I continued. "He wants you to clear up everything that is questionable."

"Finding peace at any price is cheap," she answered. "I will take care of it."

It was again time for her to return home to feed the baby. We knelt in prayer, confident that God would surely bring to her heart the peace for which she was so hungry. But again she returned home without peace in her heart. I urged her again to ask the Holy Spirit to search her heart and point out the hindrance.

The following afternoon a crestfallen Sue arrived at our home once more, her bodily posture indicating that she had not been set free.

"Has God shown you anything else wrong in your life that He wants made right?" I asked, as she entered our home.

"What face have I to make restitution in this case?" asked the distressed woman. "When I was attending the girls' school in Shanghai, because my finances were limited, one day I 'borrowed' a dollar from a wealthy classmate having no intention of ever repaying it. All of these years I have never once thought of the subject. But last night my dishonesty came to me with disturbing force. I had in a polite manner stolen a dollar from her. After she left school she married a wealthy architect. He is now carrying on a successful business in a northern city. They do not need that dollar. If I sent it to them, they would be insulted. Surely God cannot be asking that of me."

"It appears that God is speaking to you about the importance of absolute integrity," I reasoned. "He has some purpose in bringing it to your remembrance at this time. Though they may not have use for the money, if you explain clearly why you are restoring it, this will give you opportunity to witness to them that Christians must live a life that is crystal clear before the Lord and before men. Since neither of them is a Christian, this would be a good time to remind them that the Chinese evangelist, Dr. John Sung, is now in their city conducting a citywide crusade and urge them to go and hear him."

A distressed Sue sat silently and meditated on this "lose face" problem which God was manifestly asking her to rectify. It was contrary to every natural impulse to confess such a thing.

"I will go home and write the letter," she finally said. "Since money in those days was so much more valuable than now, I will send her five dollars. That will surely cover my debt."

After we prayed together, Sue set out for home. She sat in the ricksha condemning herself all the way for being so foolish when she was in school as to borrow the dollar which would put her in such a difficult place years later. What would her classmate think of her?

The following afternoon a radiant Sue arrived at our home. She was so happy that she did not even wait to knock but walked right into the house.

"I couldn't wait to get here to tell you the good news," she called. "Last evening I wrote the letter, enclosing the five dollars, and sent a servant to take it right off to the post office without delay. Before I went

113

to bed I again knelt in prayer. The Lord showed me several other places where I had been wrong, and I promised Him that I would take care of them. Then I went to bed and slept. In the middle of the night I awakened and lay there quietly thinking and praying. Suddenly it seemed that the Lord spoke to me and said, 'Sue, don't dig up those old sins any more. They are all covered by the blood of Christ.' Immediately a deep peace and joy came to my heart. I knew I was a child of God. All my old doubts about the reality of God were gone forever. I just had to come today to tell you."

Several weeks later Sue received a reply from her classmate which comforted her heart. When the classmate and her husband received the letter of confession, they could not understand Sue's motive in returning the money. As they discussed it together they decided to go and hear Dr. John Sung to find why Christians were so honest. After hearing Dr. Sung preach several times, they both became Christians. Later they erected a church in their city which was used as a place of worship when other churches were closed during World War II.

As soon as Sue and her husband were saved, both became active in the work of the Lord. They removed the partition between their living room and a bedroom in order to have a place large enough to seat government officials whom they invited to attend Bible study in their home two nights each week. Among those who attended was the provincial governor, who was later baptized. His wife had found the Lord when Sue brought her to our home. Many of the intelligentsia of the city became Christians through these home meetings.

It was a common practice for Ernest and Sue to invite prominent Chinese leaders to their home for a feast and at the same time invite missionaries and

Chinese pastors to discuss the meaning of Christianity with these who otherwise might never hear the gospel. Not a few found the Lord through this ministry. Many of their guests were impressed that this family could hold such a prominent government position and yet never serve cigarettes or wine at their feasts.

One day when Ernest took his financial report for the month to the provincial treasurer, who was notorious for his loose morals and questionable business practices, the treasurer said to him, "What is this item 'interest' that you have recorded here as a receipt?"

"This is interest which accrued from unused public funds which I deposited in the bank," Ernest answered.

"Interest!" scorned the treasurer. "Who ever heard of a public official turning in the interest on funds he has invested? You are just too good. Ernest, let me tell you what I predict about your future. I predict that your government career will end in ten months."

Embarrassed at the suggestion that hereafter he practice dishonesty, Ernest left the provincial treasurer's office fully determined that if this was the price he would have to pay to be a public servant, he would resign.

Seven months later he came to our home, "I have come to ask special prayer from you two. This morning I received a telegram asking me to report at once to the central government in Nanking. I cannot imagine what is wanted of me. But I will need your prayers."

We knelt in earnest prayer that God would guide him. If he had been misrepresented and was to be censured, that God would vindicate him; if he were to be promoted, that in this he would continue to glorify God.

Late one evening a week later he again appeared

115

at our door. Of course we were anxious to know what had happened.

"They called me into the office and said, 'We have been watching the reports that come in from your province and have been impressed by your integrity. We need men like you to care for matters of state. We have invited you here to ask you to take over the position of treasurer of your province. The present incumbent is notorious for his corruption. Go and think it over and let us know if you will accept this important position.'

" 'What does this position include?' I asked.

" 'Together with caring for all provincial funds,' they replied, 'we will expect you to take charge of the sale of lottery tickets. Yours is not one of our wealthy provinces, but this will bring in large sums of money to the central government. Let us know your answer tomorrow!' "

"After praying over the matter I felt that I should assume the work of treasurer, but I was restrained from taking over the sale of the lottery tickets. To me that is a form of gambling even though some governments use it as a source of income. That night I called on a missionary friend in the city and asked his advice. His opinion concurred with mine. After prayer with him, I was sure that I had my answer. I would accept the office of provincial treasurer, but it would be necessary for the government to find someone else to manage the sale of lotteries.

"When I gave my reply the following day, they finally agreed to my conditions though they regretted that I would not take over the lottery. They then appointed me the treasurer of this province.. I should have sent a telegram informing the provincial government of the time of arrival and they would have sent a band and black government cars, flying welcome banners, to meet me at the railroad station and escort me to my new office; but I feel that my real accession to office should be here in your house. May we kneel together in prayer, and you ask God to use me in this higher position so that many more through me may find the Savior?"

Again God vindicated His child. The former treasurer who predicted that Ernest would last ten months in the government was dismissed and Ernest took over his position.

After moving into a larger residence, Ernest and Sue immediately prepared to continue Christian services in the new home. For several years, one or more evenings each week Christians brought their friends of the upper strata of society to this home and many believed in Christ.

When the enemy forces occupied his province, Ernest refused to serve the puppet government. There was need for a man of principle to take over the treasurer's work in a wealthy province of southwest China, so the national government appointed Ernest to this work. In this new city he and Sue again opened their home for Christian services, and God blessed their efforts for Him there.

World War II was now ravaging the country. All coastal ports of China were closed by the enemy. The only supplies that could reach the country came up the Burma Road and were then flown "over the hump" to southwest China from which they were distributed over the whole unoccupied territory by truck. Most of the bulk cotton, cloth, and gauze used throughout the entire nation had to be flown in "over the hump." The government nationalized the cotton monopoly which used one-seventh of the national budget.

Where could they find a man who was honest and could resist all the temptations to corruption that such an office could present? Since all cotton products were strictly rationed, it would be easy for some in charge of the program to make themselves rich by selling cotton commodities on the black market at government expense. Again national government authorities moved Ernest and his family to the wartime capital to assume this responsible position in the central government. Ernest appointed honest men as leaders in each province and thus eliminated much of the possibility of black marketing.

Since the wartime capital was subjected to frequent raids from the enemy, many of the officials and their families lived in the suburbs of the capital. Several prominent Christians, along with Ernest's family, lived in one of these suburbs. They felt that they should erect and operate a Christian elementary and high school. Each family contributed money for the erection of a building which had a large auditorium in which religious services were held in the evening and on Sundays.

Devout Christian teachers and personnel operated a school with a high scholastic standard and a strong Christian emphasis. Many young people found the Lord in their school days and in later years became leaders in their country or in the church. Summer Bible conferences were also held at the school at which time many students and adults accepted Christ as their Savior or were led into a deeper Christian experience.

When the war ended, the central government moved the capital back to Nanking. Ernest and his family returned together with other government officials. As soon as cotton goods were no longer rationed, he asked to be relieved of national government responsibility so that he could give his full time to the work of the Christian school which had been moved to a city not far from Nanking. His request was granted.

Now he was free to carry out a desire that he and Sue had entertained for a long time, giving full time to the service of the Lord. Her father's joy knew no bounds as he heard the good news. God had answered his prayers of many years before when he dedicated Sue to the work of the Lord. When old age forced Sue's father to retire from the evangelistic field, he spent his last days in her home, witnessing to the many who came there of the power of Christ to set men free from sin.

When the communist troops occupied mainland China, shortly after the close of World War II, Ernest and Sue chose to remain there and do what they could to help people find the true God and also to encourage Christians to keep true to God in the face of cruel persecution. At first the Christian school was permitted to remain open, but later it was forced to close. After that, both Sue and Ernest suffered intensely from lack of physical comforts. Sue developed tuberculosis and went to be with her Lord whom she had served so faithfully. Ernest followed soon afterward. Their lives were not wasted. Throughout the world today there are many Chinese Christian leaders who were led to the Lord through their faithful efforts for Christ.

SOLOMON

BORN AGAIN IN AN AIR RAID

"How lucky I am!" exclaimed Mr. Shan when one July day in 1894 the midwife announced to him that his wife had borne him a third son. "I know what his name will be. We will call him Solomon. We already have two older sons. Now we have a perfect trio."

He was not so happy when the midwife gave him a bucket containing the placenta which he must take out to their field and bury. That was the duty of the father. But having completed the unpleasant task, he was pleased when he returned to have the midwife place the gangling baby, wrapped in a warm blue quilt into his arms for him to hold and enjoy. He held him tightly as he examined carefully his regular features. To manifest his delight, he rubbed noses with the baby and repeatedly shook him gently, trying to waken him.

Months later a middleman from another part of Peking came to the Shan home. A friend of similar social and economic status to the Shans had a daughter, Purity, now three years old, who had not yet been betrothed to anyone. Would the Shans be willing to consider an engagement of their third son to Purity? If so, would they find a middleman to represent them who would investigate their family and their circumstances?

The Shans approached a neighbor who was willing

to assume this responsibility. The two middlemen met and discussed a reasonable dowry for Purity. She was more valuable than some, being three years older, which would permit an earlier marriage because she would then be old enough to take responsibility for the new home. After several discussions between the two middlemen and then reporting back to the respective families, a suitable sum was agreed upon. Soon after this arrangement the parents of Solomon and Purity along with the two middlemen met at a restaurant for the engagement feast where both families signed and sealed the documents that engaged their two children.

Purity knew nothing of her engagement. She continued playing with the other children on the street and having a good time. She was short and plump with a rosy complexion. All of the neighborhood children liked her because she was so congenial, refusing to quarrel with any of them.

One day when she was about six years old her mother called her to come into the house. Hopping and skipping, she left her playmates and ran in. What was her dismay to find that her mother and her older brother's wife were preparing to bind her feet. She knew what agony this would cause her from reports of her older playmates. Her mother had a basin of warm water, soap, and two rolls of strong muslin bandages on a bench near the brick bed.

After washing her feet thoroughly they cut her toenails and let Purity lie on the bed. The sister-in-law took one foot at a time in her hand and, pressing the outside of her foot down and under as hard as her strength would allow, tried to bend the toes under the foot. Although the pain was excruciating, Purity extended her foot toward her sister-in-law, because she wanted to have small feet. She desired to be like all the other girls in the city and they had small feet.

Purity was happy to begin the process now while she was small so that when the time of her wedding rolled around, her tiny feet would please her husband. Though she screamed out in pain when the pressure was put on her feet, she continued to extend her feet toward them.

As the sister-in-law compressed her feet, her mother bound them quickly and as tightly as she could with the strong muslin bandage. Mother pulled the bandage with all her strength, wrapping it around her feet and ankles and then fastened the end by tucking it underneath the tight bandage. Of course, Purity did not run outside to play that day nor for many days to follow. In fact, for the rest of her life she would be crippled because of her bound feet and would never walk normally again.

She sat on the bed for the remainder of that day hugging her pain. When necessary to walk, she held onto the furniture for support and stubbed along on her heels. It seemed as though she could not endure the pain and the numbness in her feet. The circulation in her feet had practically stopped.

A week later, when Purity had just succeeded in learning to walk a short distance on her bound feet, once more she had to lie on the bed while her mother and sister-in-law removed the bandages and then, before the circulation started up again, pulled the bandages even tighter than they had been the previous week. Once more she screamed out in pain, but again she pushed her foot forward while they drew the bandages tighter. This procedure became a weekly occurrence. The rosy color gradually disappeared from her cheeks, and she became thinner and thinner. There was never an hour, day or night, when she was free of pain.

After several months had passed, she could feel a throbbing in her feet. In her childish ignorance, she thought that it was a part of the process of footbinding.

But when the pain became so severe that she could not stand on her feet, her mother began to investigate the cause. It was just as she had feared. The long toenails, which had not been cut for some months, were causing infected sores on the soles of her feet. Her mother had her soak her feet in hot water to cleanse away the pus. But immediately afterward she rebound them as tightly as possible. The process was repeated daily until the sores finally healed. After that experience they were more careful to cut her nails more frequently. The problem recurred more than once.

Purity never attended school. One brother had a teacher come to the home to give him private lessons on memorizing the classics and writing characters, along with adding, subtracting, multiplying, and dividing on the abacus. Since a girl went to live at her husband's home when she got married, it was not considered necessary for her to learn to read and write. Purity grew up never learning to recognize characters or to write. She sat for hours each day learning to weave cloth on the family loom. She spent time embroidering shoes, pillow tops, and fancy squares for the sleeve bands of her father's coats. Her mother also taught her to cook and to make clothing. She was so short for her age that everyone called her "The Little Girl."

When Solomon was nearing his sixteenth birthday, his parents visited an astrologer to inquire which was the auspicious day for the wedding of the third son. They carried with them the dates of the birthdays of the two young people concerned. The astrologer examined the signs of the zodiac in which both were born, compared them with the movement of the stars, and then wrote the auspicious wedding date on a sheet of scarlet paper.

Mr. Shan had the middleman take it to the girl's middleman who, in turn, delivered it to the girl's family. There was excitement accompanied by loud talking among all members of her family. Purity would soon be married.

On the wedding day both households were beehives of activity long before daylight. Purity's boxes of clothing and bedding were made ready to go. Her mother had to force her to put on her wedding clothes. It was customary for the bride to show her grief at leaving her home by refusing to cooperate with her parents in dressing for the wedding. When they finally got her dressed in her scarlet satin embroidered skirt, overhanging satin blouse and scarlet shoes and had a sprig of artificial flowers in her well-oiled hair, she presented a lovely picture. Her heart beat fast at the thought of seeing her husband for the first time. She sat on the bed with bowed head as she waited for him to arrive, her face covered with a heavy red muslim veil.

The six-foot groom looked attractive in his navy blue silk gown topped with a black silk short jacket. Over his black, oiled hair he wore a black satin beanie cap, finished with a red ball on the top. His queue extended well down his back. He had difficulty jack-knifing into the sedan chair carried by two men.

In response to the middleman's knock, the father opened the gate and invited the groom into the house. The women served him small sponge cakes, peanuts, watermelon seeds, and dainty bowls of hot tea. Purity remained back in her bedroom weeping at the thought of leaving home. When no one was looking, she stole sly glances at the groom. She was shocked at how tall and lanky he looked. She wondered if he would hate her because she was so short. It was obvious that she could stand under his outstretched arm.

After the middleman and Solomon had partaken of

the delicacies and hot tea provided for them, the middleman said to his host, "It is time for us to return. Is the bride ready?"

"I will go and see," replied her father. He came to the doorway of her bedroom and called through the curtain, "Is she ready?" Her mother and matron of honor were beside her trying to convince her that she should go along with her husband. But she continued to weep as she showed her unwillingness to leave home. When they tried to force her to arise she resisted with all her might.

After about a half hour of this conduct they succeeded in getting her to stand on her tiny feet, bound so tightly for the occasion that she could hardly walk. With effort they forced her into the living room where the groom was waiting for her. Her face was still covered with the thick red muslin veil which she grasped.

The groom was shocked to see how short she was, but it was improper for him to gaze very long at her or to take her arm to help her into the sedan chair. His middleman urged him to return to his sedan chair, the first in the line, and sit there until someone could seat his bride in the red-draped one prepared for her just behind him.

Mrs. Shan came to the gate to meet her. Purity cooperated with the matron of honor as she escorted her into the yard, because she must not irritate her mother-in-law by showing any unwillingness to come into her home. She was led into the guest room where Solomon had already taken his place facing the family idol shrine, and she took her place beside him. The master of ceremonies faced the crowd of relatives and friends who pushed their way into the room after the bride. Immediately the ceremony began.

"Let the bride and groom bow to the God of heaven and earth," called the master of ceremonies.

The two young people kowtowed. Purity found it difficult to get up again because of her painful feet. The matron of honor helped her.

"Let the bride and groom bow to the ancestors and to the family idols," he shouted again.

Once more the bride and groom prostrated themselves.

"Let the bride and groom bow three times to the father and mother of the groom," came the third command. "One bow! Two bows! Three bows!" Both of them cooperated.

"Let the bride and groom face each other," he called again.

The matron of honor swung the timid bride around so that she faced her husband. With effort she threw back the red muslin veil from the face of the bride.

"Isn't she pretty?" called out someone among the crowd of guests and bystanders.

"One bow!" called the master of ceremonies.

The matron of honor pushed Purity's head down in a forced bow to her husband, while the crowd snickered.

"Two bows!" came another call. .

Again Purity made a forced bow while the groom bowed to her.

"Three bows!" he called again.

The guests snickered. To them the bowing was the wedding ceremony. They were really man and wife now.

"Let the bride and groom face the bride's parents and give them three bows," he shouted.

Her parents came from the crowd and stood in front of them while they received their three ceremonial bows, then returned to their place in the crowd.

"Let the bride and the groom right about face, and give three bows to all of the guests who have taken

127

time from their work to attend the wedding ceremony and have spent money on the gifts for them," the master of ceremonies called again.

The couple cooperated.

The groom then led the way to the room in the courtyard which would be their home.

The matron of honor took the bride by the arm, and forced her to follow her husband. She showed some reluctance to go, but feared to offend her mother-in-law. She must win her approval on the first day, or she would have a hard time later on. The groom disappeared into the crowd in the courtyard while others took the bride into her room and seated her on the brick bridal bed.

Then the guests were seated, eight at a table. The bride and groom were given the place of honor in the living room just under the shelf containing the idols and ancestral tablets. The bride's parents and relatives were also seated there. Until it was time for the hot food to be served, all guests busied themselves with visiting, eating peanuts, or cracking open seeds with their teeth and throwing the skins on the floor.

The bride refused to eat anything. Custom demanded that she eat nothing for two days to show her homesickness for her parents. On the third day she must return to visit them.

Next morning she arose as soon as she heard anyone stirring and went to the kitchen to help prepare breakfast. From now on she would be the servant in the home while her mother-in-law relaxed or carried around the grandchildren.

Life was not happy for the young bride. Solomon found a good position in the accounting department of a railroad company. Having plenty of money to spend, he developed habits of drinking wine and smoking both tobacco and opium. Well-dressed and stylish, he was popular with the young set with whom he associated.

Mrs. Shan kept watching for the day when her third son would present her with a grandson. The two older brothers had both sons and daughters. Why did Purity have no children? Then she began to taunt Purity about it until she made her life miserable. There was nothing further Purity could do to give birth to a son.

One day Mrs. Shan called Solomon to her room and talked with him confidentially about the disgrace of a family not having children. Did not an ancient Chinese sage say, "There are three things which are unfilial, and to have no posterity is the greatest of them." Moreover, it was common practice when the first wife bore no children for the husband to take another one who could. Solomon was having a good time without children and was not impressed with her suggestion. But when she continued to press him to take another wife, he finally consented to his parents' choosing one for him. Purity did not object because she had suffered enough by their daily taunts about her barrenness. She was not allowed to forget that the family was disgraced by her childlessness.

The second bride was brought to the home with a simple ceremony. She was given a room beside Purity's. Normally the two wives hate each other and vie with each other to win the husband's affections. Purity decided that it would be to her advantage to accept her fate and make friends with the concubine. They talked together, worked together, and acted like real sisters. When Solomon's office was moved from Peking farther south, he took both of his wives with him. In a new environment away from his parents, all three began to give themselves to careless living. They especially enjoyed smoking opium together and sleeping out their pleasant dreams. When neither wife produced any children, the second brother of the family gave Solomon one of his sons who would care for him in his old age.

In 1937 war broke out between China and Japan. Railroads, cities, and army installations were bombed by the enemy. As the Japanese took over section after section of the railroad, Solomon soon found himself without work. Because rail lines were cut, he and his wives could not return to Peking, which was now in enemy hands. They fled to northwest China to get away from bombings. It was not long after they reached there until he found a good accounting position with Mr. Chang, whom he had known in Peking.

He rented a house in which he and his wives practiced the daily use of opium. At that time the Chinese government became strict with the many opium offenders and took steps to force users to break the habit. Solomon and his wives did not want to quit. Though some of their friends went to opium-cure hospitals, Solomon and his household refused to go.

It was at this time that Mr. Chang became a Christian and was instantly delivered from all of his evil habits, including opium. He had separated from his concubine when he was baptized. He held early morning Christian meetings in his office which he expected all of his employees to attend. Then each evening he had preaching services in his home. Solomon could not escape the meetings in the office, but he refused to attend those in Chang's home. He could not but marvel, however, at the remarkable change in the life of his employer. There was evidently a power in Christianity, but he would have nothing to do with it. Buddhism had been the religion of his ancestors for centuries, and it would be his religion.

One evening as he and his wives were experiencing an opium seance, the anti-opium authorities walked into their home, arrested all three, and took them off to prison where they kept them for a month. During those days Solomon did a lot of serious thinking. Imprisonment was a terrible disgrace. They ought to change. But opium had too firm a grip on them to break the habit in their own strength. In fact, he realized that he had not too much longer to live if he continued the use of the drug. He and his second wife were already so emaciated and had such sallow complexions that they were frightened when they saw themselves in a mirror. But not one of the three had enough willpower to stop. They were held in the cruel grip of an expensive habit.

Meanwhile, the change in his employer, through belief in Jesus Christ, kept recurring in his thinking. Could Christ make the same change in him? Would he have to send his second wife away if he should believe in Christ? Where could she go? Would her parents bring legal proceedings against him for divorcing their daughter without cause? His thoughts were in a whirl as he pondered over and over how he could extricate himself from his dilemma.

When the month in prison was ended, the three returned to their home with the warning that they would receive much more severe punishment if they were caught again. Execution was even hinted. Solomon returned to his accounting position and to the morning preaching services.

Just at that time I was holding meetings in that city, staying in Mr. Chang's home. One midmorning, Solomon came to the home to discuss company business with Chang. Chang was away; only the woman who did the cooking, my infant son, and I were home. Solomon had no more than entered the door of the home when a loud alarm split the air, warning the people that enemy planes were headed in our direction. Normally everyone ran to a huge dugout in the city wall two blocks away and waited there

131

until the all-clear sounded. Air raids were a wearisome wait for both children and adults. Sometimes it was four to eight hours before the all-clear sounded and people were allowed on the streets again.

"I'm not going to run for shelter," said Solomon. "I will stay right here until it is all over."

"Neither am I running anywhere," said the cook. "I have too much to do to sit inside that city wall half a day and endure hunger and thirst."

I agreed. "The baby is better off here than in that shelter. Let's just sit down here at home and trust the Lord to keep the planes from our area."

In my previous contacts with Solomon, though he had always been courteous, he let it be known that he was definitely not interested in any "Western religion." But I felt that today God had given this opportunity free from business distractions when I could talk quietly with him and find out his objections to Christianity. I slipped into my bedroom to pray and then returned with my Chinese Bible.

"Solomon," I began, "you have attended some of the meetings in your office and have heard us tell about the Christian religion. You have seen some of the changed lives. What is your opinion of what you have seen and heard?"

"It is good," he replied, giving a characteristic nod of his head.

"Would you like to have Jesus save you?" I went on.

"Yes," he replied without hesitation.

I was surprised at his immediate affirmative reply. Was he using his usual politeness to save the missionary's face, or was God answering prayer?

"Have you any questions about your giving your life to Jesus?" I continued.

"No, none at all," he replied.

"Would you be willing to kneel here in this living

132

room and ask God to come to your heart today?" I asked.

"Yes," was his abrupt reply.

"All right, let's kneel right here and pray," I said.

Following my short prayer, Solomon began to pray and tell God what a sinner he had been. He confessed that he was being crushed in the jaws of his evil habits from which he could not extricate himself and he asked the Lord to come into his heart then and there.

I opened my Bible to Matthew 7:7 and let him read, "Ask and it will be given to you; seek and you will find; knock and the door will be opened to you."

"Do you believe this promise from God's Word?" I asked.

"Yes, I do," he replied. "I believe that Jesus has come to me today. I feel His power in my life. I feel like a new man."

His conversion was that simple. He had counted the cost of discipleship and had decided to trust Christ to take control of his life. He was determined to forsake all sin forever with God's help.

Together we looked into the Word of God until the all-clear sounded. He hurried back to the office to tell the employees the good news. That evening when he returned to his home, he burst into the house telling his wives that God had saved him and that, with God's help, he was through with sin forever. He smashed his opium lamp, burned his cigarettes, and showed them the Bible that Chang had given him. That evening he began reading it consecutively.

Solomon invited his wives to attend the evening services with him. Purity decided to do so, but the second wife said, "You won't find me going there. You may accept this religion if you like, but I want nothing to do with it." She felt painfully insecure. She was far away from family and friends. Would her husband send her away as Mr. Chang had done to his concubine? Where could she go? How could she support herself? These questions weighed upon her mind day and night.

Purity soon found the Lord. Opium and other habits disappeared. As if in testimony to the new freedom she had in Christ, she loosened the wrappings around her feet; however, because in childhood the bones had been broken, she still needed some support from bandages. As the two Christians prayed together in the home, the second wife became increasingly hungry for this same peace and joy that the others had; but she would not betray her feelings. When they left for church, she stayed at home. How left out and alone she felt!

The Christian women from the church went and called on her, urging her to let Jesus into her heart, but she consistently refused. She wanted nothing to do with this new religion. Then one day when some of the Christian women called in the home and asked if they might pray with her, she replied, "Yes, if you would like to, but don't ask me to pray yet."

As they prayed, her tears began to flow. She had wanted for a long time to let Christ into her heart but feared the consequences if she did so. When the others finished praying, they urged her to pray. Suddenly she broke out in supplication to God. It was a short prayer but sincere and earnest. She knew soon that Christ had come to her. She was changed after that.

She and Purity called in many homes to tell of Christ's saving power. She began to learn to read her Bible and made rapid progress. She attended all services at the church and grew in grace and in knowledge of her Lord and Savior Jesus Christ. One day as she knelt in prayer before the Lord, she was filled with the Holy Spirit. From that time on, she had power to testify to others and to win them to the Lord as she had not known before.

But how were they to solve their marital problem? They talked it over together. Since the second wife had no other home to go to, it was decided that she would remain with them as before but that she and Solomon would live as brother and sister, rather than as husband and wife. From that time forward, they called her Younger Sister. Solomon felt that he had an obligation to support and protect her. Theirs was a happy home where Christ's presence dwelt. God made each of them a sharp tool in His kingdom. Purity had great power in prayer; the Younger Sister was a keen personal worker. God restored health to their bodies which had been ravaged by opium.

The war with Japan ended but the struggle between the Nationalists and the communists continued with the latter making steady gains. As communist troops neared his city, Mr. Chang closed up his business and disbanded the employees. He caught a plane to Taiwan, hoping that unsettled conditions would soon pass over and he could return. But the opportunity never came. Solomon, Purity, Younger Sister, and a nephew and his family were able to get space on the last flight out of their city before the communist drive closed the airport. They too were able to reach Taiwan. Younger Sister soon was in demand as a Bible woman going from house to house and working among the women there. For nearly twenty years, she lived in a northern city, helping in church work, leading women's meetings, and doing personal evangelism with women in their homes.

Solomon and Purity lived in the southern part of Taiwan, where to their joy they encountered the same group of missionaries who had led Solomon to the Lord in northwest China. We had been looking for someone to help in the transaction of business and legal matters. Where could we find anyone more suitable than this well-trained Chinese businessman?

Solomon took over the business matters for the mission which foreigners find so difficult in a strange land. Besides this he conducted church services, acted as secretary and treasurer of the local church and annual conference, and served in many other ways. He was known in Christian circles all over the island of Taiwan as a Christian statesman. He later represented Taiwan in America in international conferences as a lay delegate from his church. He liked to refer to himself as a "brand from the burning."

Purity is still a great prayer warrior. Whenever there is a church problem or someone sick or gone astray, people still search out Purity to help pray the problem to a solution. All three continued to serve the Lord joyfully even when they were somewhat restricted by the infirmities of old age.

Chapter Nine

MARK

FOUNDER OF THE BACK-TO-JERUSALEM BAND

"What kind of creature is that standing on our street?" exclaimed Mark, a teenaged schoolboy, on his way home from school one autumn afternoon. All of the schoolchildren automatically came to an abrupt stop as they gazed in awe. As they walked closer to observe, different ones excitedly called out, "It has pink skin."

"Look at the golden hair showing from under the black head scarf."

"Its eyes are blue. Look at those big feet. It must be a man."

"She is a foreign devil," explained a passerby who overheard their remarks. "Don't you know that these foreign devils have come here to tell us about their Western gods? Women over in their countries have big feet just like our men."

The children surrounded missionary Mary Schlosser as she went on with her sermon about the Son of God who came from heaven to die on the cross in the place of sinful man to save him from his sins.

Mark listened long enough to discover that she was talking the local Chinese dialect. Then off he ran at top speed to invite his parents to come and see the strange sight.

"Ma! Ma!" he shouted as he pushed open the door of their home. "Come quick, and see the foreign devil down the street telling about her foreign god. She can tell good stories in our language. I just heard her tell a good one.''

His mother beat the flour off her hip-length black jacket and started down the street behind him. The crowd was increasing by the minute as school children reached more and more homes. Though it was time to get the evening meal, Mark and his mother listened until the end of the sermon. When the missionary invited any who desired to worship this Jesus of whom she was speaking to come into the little store just back of where she stood, a few went inside the building to hear more; but Mark and his mother went on home. She was impressed by what she heard, but because for generations their family had worshiped idols and ancestors, she would not adopt a new religion without careful investigation. Day after day she attended the meetings.

Then one day when Mark's mother was convinced that Mrs. Schlosser was telling about a living God and not a dead one like her family idols, she went into the little store-chapel, followed instructions on how to seek God, and that very day Jesus saved her. Later, as more of the neighbors believed in Jesus, regular services were held in the little chapel. Mark enjoyed sitting on one of the front benches, lustily singing the hymns. Idol-burning ceremonies were held in many homes where both parents had become Christians. This caused a wave of persecution of believers.

As the Christians walked along the streets, they were subjected to cries of ''Followers of the foreign devils,'' ''Ancestor burners,'' ''Rejectors of ancestors,'' ''Worshipers of foreign gods,'' ''Haters of ancestors.''

Mark was embarrassed to be the butt of his neighbors' ridicule and decided that he would never attend another Christian service.

When Sunday morning rolled around, his mother

called to him, "Mark, come along. It is time for church."

"I am not going anymore," he replied. "I am tired of being called a foreign devil. You may believe in Jesus if you desire, but I am through."

Ignoring Mark's protests his father called, "Come and get on your new padded coat. It is time for us to be on our way."

"I hate the girlish coat," Mark fussed. "None of the other boys are wearing flowered coats anymore. Haven't you seen that boys are now wearing black coats cut in Western style? I don't want to look like a girl."

Mark was adamant. He wanted nothing to do with the new religion. He pled to remain at home while his parents and older sister went to church. But his parents would not concede to him. They forced him to put on the hated long gown. Then, with one parent on each side holding his hands, they pulled an unwilling, balking boy down the street to the chapel while his classmates and friends looked on laughing. He kept remonstrating, "I hate church. I hate this long gown." But every Sunday he was forced to go.

The church had opened a Christian boys' school two days' journey from their home. Because Mark created such a scene when taken to the local church, his parents decided to send him away to this Christian school. He was glad to get away from home where he was being forced to attend church services. He thought that if he could get to a boarding school, no one could force him to go to church if he did not want to go.

The Christian school administrators found that Mark had a keen mind. Since his parents were Christians, he was admitted to the school. From his first day in school, he made it clear to everyone that, though he desired an education, he wanted nothing to do with Christianity. He attended morning chapel and evening prayers with the rest of his classmates because they were compulsory; but he went only to cause trouble.

When others knelt in prayer, he would reach under the seat and pull someone's leg, snatch off a shoe, or pinch the seat of some boy's pants. While the preaching was going on, he would either pull someone's hair or stick him with a pin just to create a disturbance. Scholastically, he was an excellent student, receiving the highest grades in his class. But wherever he was, there was trouble. At one time the staff considered recommending sending him home, but one member interceded for him saying, "It will be a sad reflection on us if we cannot control a child from a Christian family. For the parents' sake, we should allow him to remain and all of us continue to pray for him that God will change him." And remain he did.

Mark was daily troubled with the thought that he was being forced to accept a pattern of life which he abhorred. He reflected on the way his ancestors had lived.

His grandfather, a well-known official in the area, had lived as he pleased. In later life he had committed some misdemeanors which were examined and for which he was convicted. For these offenses he had been taken outside the city wall and beheaded. His relatives, not wanting to bury him in disgrace because he lacked a part of his body, had asked a goldsmith to make a gold head with which they buried him.

Mark also had an uncle who had been permitted to choose his own pattern of life. True, it was not the most desirable type of life, but he had at least been permitted to make his own choice. As a young man the uncle and his companions had developed profligate ways of living. At first he indulged only in drinking and smoking. But later he began to use opium. As the appetite increased, the amount of money needed for purchasing opium also increased. In order to get cash he gradually sold off the family jewels and treasures. When they were gone, he went out one night and secretly robbed his grandfather's grave of the gold head and exchanged it for opium. Later he sold off chests of family heirlooms but, because selling them box by box consumed too much time, he sold them a room at a time to buy opium to satisfy his appetite. After he had sold much of the family land, he succumbed to his appetite.

Mark recalled how the other heirs had been reduced to a much lower standard of living because of his uncle's excesses. Mark did not plan to carry out the sins of his ancestors, but he wanted to dabble in a few of the pleasures of life without having someone tell him constantly that to do so is sin. He longed for the time when he could finish the Christian high school and be on his own where he could make his own decisions. Why did his parents adopt this Western religion which was so different from that followed by all of his ancestors? He longed for his freedom.

Then in 1927 and 1928 Chiang Kai-shek's conquering armies unified the country that had been plagued by ever-changing regional warlords. When the war began to approach the province where the Christian Boys' School was located, the faculty felt that they should not take responsibility for all of these young men away from home and disbanded the school. Mark succeeded in finishing his high school course and then went off on his own to find some opportunity for further education. To his delight, he found a military school which was slanted toward communism. The school advocated the dismissal of all foreigners from China and strongly opposed the Christian church. He had at last found a group whose views harmonized with his own, and for a year he was an apt pupil. When this course was finished, he fled to an eastern province in order to avoid the fighting armies.

In this coastal province, he found a newly-formed organization that advocated the education of peasants. In the past, by custom, usually only the eldest son in each family had been educated to care for all family correspondence and business. But the group that he now joined advocated the education of all men and boys in a family. It was the beginning of the public school movement in China. The leader organized a school which trained young men to go into all the villages, call the men together, and sell the program to them. If interest was sufficient, they then set up schools for illiterates in temples or other public buildings. Each proponent of the plan was given an excellent training in public speaking before he was allowed to go out into the country to enlist students.

Mark went into this training with all the zest he could muster. He was sure that this type of education was what China needed. He listened carefully as the teacher told them how to prepare their speeches, which embodied much of the propaganda material that they were given in class. Following the delivery of the speech, the teacher and fellow-students would make criticisms and help the student make corrections. Mark thought that it would not be necessary for him to write out his speech. He had natural eloquence upon which he depended when he had his facts well in mind.

When it came his turn to make a speech, Mark decided to use a flowery opening sentence from the Chinese Classics as an introduction and then present the arguments for the "Every Man Literate" program. He stepped up onto the platform with much self-confidence. But when he faced that large auditorium full of fellow students, stage fright seized him.

With a loud, clear voice and careful articulation, he repeated an expressive proverb from the Classics. When that was finished, he could not think of one other thing to say. He cleared his throat and repeated the same sentence from Confucius. Still his mind was blank. He cleared his throat again and waited a moment for something else to follow. But nothing came. For the third time he began with the proverb from Confucius. His mind was still blank. Blushing profusely, he walked down from the platform and took his seat. Mortified beyond words, he waited to hear the devastating criticism his professor would make before all his classmates.

After what seemed an endless pause, he heard it. "That speech had a tiger's head and a snake's tail, young man. I hope that you have learned your lesson. Never again appear before a group until you have memorized every word of your speech. Depending on natural eloquence or the inspiration of the moment will get you nowhere."

Mark wished he could vanish into a hole. He knew that the professor's rebuke was warranted. As soon as he returned to his room, he began preparation for a second speech. Never again would he repeat this first performance. After he had written out the entire speech, he went out on a hillside to practice it. He put all of his persuasive powers and his elocution to work to convince his audience of the need for universal education of males in the land. Over and over he repeated his lecture to his stone audience until he was sure that he had it thoroughly in hand. At the close of the course, he was chosen among other students to go out into the country to put the program across.

Back home his parents were concerned about their son. He had now reached marriageable age, and they wanted to choose a wife for him. On one of his trips home, they suggested a girl to him, but he spurned their offer.

"Let me take care of my own marriage," he said. "Other men are making their own choices now without consulting their parents. Please let me find a girl of my own choice. I can tell you one thing. She will not be a Christian. I had enough of that when I was younger."

The grieved parents said no more. Daily they took the matter to the Lord in prayer.

Mark found a girl in an official family who could read simple booklets and write ordinary characters. She had never attended a Christian service. When the middleman suggested her to him, he said, "I haven't many requirements for the woman who will be my wife, but I have one stipulation. She must not be a Christian. That is my one demand."

"Oh, I can guarantee that she is no Christian," replied the go-between. They became engaged. After Mark set the wedding date, his mother came to the city where the fianceé lived to help prepare for the wedding.

"I am planning a church wedding for you according to Christian custom," she announced to Mark.

"No, I am planning a traditional Chinese wedding," he replied.

Together they battled it out for some time. In the end he agreed that he would be married in the church so that his parents could have it their way for their friends, but immediately afterward he would have a traditional wedding elsewhere to which he would invite his friends.

At the time of the Christian ceremony, Mark walked down the aisle looking neither to the right nor to the left, with his chin firmly set in a more-determined-than-ever pose. He was satisfied that he was a filial son who had let his parents have their way. But as soon as the feast with the Christians was over, he went to another place and had a traditional Chinese wedding with his friends where he served the customary liquor and cigarettes and burned incense to the idols.

Immediately after the wedding, according to Chinese custom, he took his wife to his parents' home where she could perform her obligation as a daughter-in-law by waiting on her new father and mother and adapting to their way of living. He himself had to return to his educational work in the eastern province.

Mark's mother realized that this was her God-given opportunity to introduce her daughter-in-law to Jesus Christ. Daily they had her participate in family prayers. The new bride liked all that she saw and heard about this new religion. It seemed much more sensible to her than Buddhism. Meanwhile, her mother-in-law thought of a better plan. She would see if they would accept her daughter-in-law into the Bible school where she could both improve her reading and also understand the gospel better. She was accepted at the school, where she enjoyed all that she heard. But she hesitated about praying because she knew that Mark would become very angry if she became a Christian. She remembered only too well that he had wanted a heathen wife.

When Mark heard that his wife was attending a Christian school, he became furious. He forthwith began house hunting and enlisted his friend to help him. His chief condition was that the house be as far from the Christian church as possible. Though he and his friends searched the city carefully, the only place that was available in that whole city was rooms in a courtyard immediately opposite the Christian church.

He continued searching for a place to live, but without success. He was frustrated. The longer his wife remained at the Bible school, the more she would be contaminated by this Western religion. Consequently, he decided to rent the rooms opposite the church and warn his wife that not once should she ever attend church services. He returned to his parents' home to get her.

The Chinese Christians and missionaries in the eastern province were alert to watch for new arrivals in their city. They made frequent calls on Mark's wife, inviting her to attend church services, but she dared not defy her husband and attend. When they called in the home to invite Mark to church, without hesitation he replied, "Chinese religions are good enough for me. We won't be attending the Christian church." His wife often talked with the Chinese pastor and wife at her own gateway.

A daughter and later a son were born to them, while he continued to carry on the rural education program. Mark kept busy with his school duties during the day and with his home responsibilities in the evening. He was elated when his son was born. He saw to it that his son was dressed in attractive modern clothes, and he carried him out on the street each evening so that neighbors could admire the baby. He was fond of rubbing noses with his son just to hear him chuckle. (Westerners kiss; Chinese rub noses.)

Winter gradually drew on, and winters can be severe in that coastal province. Though the mother made the children wear padded coats and trousers and wrapped the baby in a warm quilt when he went out of doors, he came down with a severe cold. They first took him to a doctor who practiced Chinese medicine. Though the anxious parents made up the prescribed bitter brew of different Chinese herbs and forced the baby to drink it, he continued to get worse. Then they

146

switched to Western medicines only to find that nothing was relieving the severe lung congestion. He continued to worsen. Both parents sat beside him, helpless to do anything to relieve his distress. His little nostrils became distended with each breath and his breathing became more and more labored. Mark was decidedly worried. The missionaries and Chinese pastor came to see them and someone suggested that if the parents would repent and believe in Jesus, God might heal their son. Mark became infuriated over this remark. Though he was normally courteous, this time he blurted out, "Will you please take care of your own affairs and let me take care of mine."

As night drew on, the worried father could remain in his home no longer. The baby was gasping for breath and was rolling his eyes until only the whites were visible. Mark could not bear to see his son die. He put on his padded overcoat and went outside to walk up and down the street. The weather was bitterly cold. Where could he go for shelter from the cold wind? Evangelistic services were in progress in the church just across the street from his home. The church was practically unheated except for a pan of red-hot charcoal burning in the center of the room where worshipers could go during the service and warm their feet occasionally to prevent freezing. He decided to go inside and sit in a back seat. He could at least escape from the bitter winds.

The Christians had been praying for the entire family that God would somehow break through into their lives. The Chinese evangelist recognized this outstanding gentleman as he came into the church that night and used his strongest arguments for Christianity. Mark became much interested in the sermon and listened attentively. In his deep concentration, he forgot that he had vowed never to attend a church service and momentarily forgot that he had left a dying

147

son at home with his wife. Many plausible arguments were given by the evangelist why men should be Christians. The Holy Spirit was taking the message home to Mark's heart. One by one all of his reasons for opposition vanished.

As soon as the sermon was ended and people were beginning to go forward to seek God, the evangelist turned the service over to the pastor while he slipped quietly to the rear of the church to ask Mark to accompany him to the belfry room. Mark did so, and together they discussed the plan of salvation and some of the promises that God had given to those who would seek Him. At the close of the talk, when asked if he would kneel in prayer, Mark quietly knelt before God. He saw his sins rise before him like a mountain. In contrition, he began to weep and to ask God to have mercy on him and forgive his many sins. He confessed his rebellion at home, his disregard of authority at school, and his planned evasion of God since he left school. He closed by saying, "Lord, I am not here repenting because my son is sick. I am making a life decision. Whether my son lives or dies, I will be a Christian." Right there God met him and saved him.

Arising from his knees, he hurried home announcing the good news to his wife, who was still walking the floor with the sick child. Together, through the night, they took turns carrying their precious son. Just before daylight the baby died. To reaffirm his commitment to Christ the grief-stricken father insisted that the child be given a Christian burial.

From that time forward Mark and his wife, who also accepted the Lord, and their little girl began attending the church services regularly. Mark's spiritual progress was so rapid and his knowledge of the Scriptures was so profound that fellow Christians could hardly believe that he had so recently been converted. He put in as much time as possible after school hours reading his Bible and praying. God gave him a remarkable understanding of the Scriptures. He went out with the pastor of the church and other Christians to hold open-air meetings. He also witnessed to his fellow teachers what God had done for him. Some laughed. But others were impressed by the change in his life.

The genuineness of the change was put to a further test not too long after he was saved. One evening all of the teachers were to have a feast together at which they could discuss rural education problems. As they passed the usual package of cigarettes to the guests, Mark declined. Someone in the group who had heard of the change in his life called out, "Mark, what are you trying to pull off? We all know that you smoke. You have always smoked your share along with the rest of us. Come on, have a smoke."

Mark replied, "It is true that I used to smoke and perhaps indulged more than the rest of you. But one night two weeks ago I became a Christian. God changed my life, and I have not smoked since. Please pardon me; I will not take any."

Another teacher came up and remonstrated, "Can't you be sociable? Being a Christian does not keep one from following social customs. Of course, you must take one."

"Not even one," replied Mark. "Since I have become a Christian, I intend to be a genuine one wherever I am. Again I ask to be excused."

Then his most intimate friend came up with a pack of cigarettes in his hand and knelt before him saying, "Now will you take one? Have you lost all regard for custom? Do you see that I have knelt to you?" (Kneeling to an individual obligates him to comply with the request.)

Mark pulled him to his feet saying, "Sorry, friend,

get up! Even if you kneel to me, I will not accept one."

Another associate tried from another angle. "Mark, here is my cigarette all lit and ready. Take just one puff and let us see that you are still one of the group. Come on, take just one puff."

Again Mark held his ground by replying, "Not even one puff. One puff is the same as smoking one cigarette or one pack. I refuse to take even one puff."

Seeing that he was immovable and would not be dissuaded, they stopped further attempts to force him. When they passed the wine around at the feast and raised the glass in a toast, again they tried to convince him that he should do as the others were doing. He replied, "I will give my toast with tea," and raised his cup of tea.

His friends left the feast that night with a deep respect for the man who could stand by his convictions without wavering.

Civil war reached that province. Those carrying on the rural education program felt that it was advisable to close down the program temporarily, disband the headquarters, and let all the workers who could return to their homes.

Mark and his family set out for his parents' home. When he reached home, he could not understand how some who called themselves Christians could be so lukewarm. The neighbors on the other hand were astonished at the change that had taken place in him. Mark took an active part in the church services, and during the week he got some of the Christians stirred up to go out in the nearby villages to hold open-air meetings. People were finding the Lord, and a lukewarm church became on fire for God.

Chinese workers and missionaries in the area could see that the hand of the Lord was upon Mark for service. He also felt that God had called him to His work. When he made application to attend the Bible school where his wife had attended for a short time after they were first married, the entire family was accepted. Mark could be in the advanced course, his wife in the preparatory department, the daughter in kindergarten and the toddling little brother, who had recently come to their home, could play in a supervised sand pile or toddlers' nursery.

The years of intensive training in the Word and in practical service slipped quickly by. One summer he and a few other students from the Bible school spent their entire vacation evangelizing in the province of Kansu. When they returned to the Bible school in the fall, Mark was convinced that God wanted him in the great northwest when he had finished his Bible school course.

During World War II, when the Japanese occupied Mark's home province, a number of Chinese Christians and missionary colleagues sensed that the time was ripe to go to the northwest. My husband and I, along with Mark's family were pioneers in this venture. We felt that the most important need of northwest China was to establish a Bible school to train young people for the Lord's work. If new churches were opened, where else would they find pastors to nurture the converts?

After we prayed for some weeks about a location, God provided premises adequate for a school. Gradually other workers joined the group. Northwest Bible Institute became a reality.

Mark and the other teachers taught in the institute during the week and frequently, over a weekend, helped other workers establish new churches or minister in existing churches. The Lord sent many fine students to Northwest Bible Institute. During the summer months when the school was closed, Mark and other faculty members went farther west into

Kansu and Tsinghai to preach the gospel in those areas. Students from these two remote provinces also came to Northwest Bible Institute for training for the Lord's work.

One Easter weekend Mark was in a city twenty miles from the institute helping to open a new work in an area that had no Christian church. Since there were only a few inquirers, he did not call the new believers together for a sunrise service on Easter morning. Instead, he himself, took his Bible and went for a quiet time with the Lord beside the river that flowed just outside the city wall. Cutting winter winds chilled him through and through. Wearing a quilted suit, a woolen sweater, and a padded overcoat, he shivered in the cold as he walked back and forth along the riverside, reading his Bible and praying.

The presence of the Lord was unusually real to him that Easter morning. God seemed to say to him, "Mark, think how the gospel has been carried in a generally westerly direction from Jerusalem on to Europe and England, then to America and finally China. China has been a hard nut for the Christian church to crack. Many missionaries have lost their lives in giving the gospel to this land. Hundreds were killed during the Boxer Uprising and since. But God has triumphed and now in all provinces in the country there are believers. I want you to look at the unreached areas between the western border of China and Jerusalem. I have left this entire region as a harvest field for the Chinese church. Kansu, Tsinghai, Tibet, Sinkiang, Nepal, Afghanistan, Iran, Iraq, Arabia — all of these I have left for the Chinese church to evangelize. I want you to stir up interest in this mission."

Mark knew that this was no ordinary voice speaking to him. All his life he had planned on spending his later years in Szechwan or some other warm climate. All of these countries mentioned had cold or arid climates which did not attract him. Tears flowed freely as God continued to show him His plan of action, causing him to realize his own inability to perform such a work. God assured him that He would be with him and provide both workers and funds to promote such a program. As he walked back to the little chapel for the Easter morning service, his whole heart was saying yes to the will of God, whatever it might mean. But how could he find workers and funds for such a vast work?

Twenty miles away at the Northwest Bible Institute on that same Easter Sunday, students who were not out on a preaching assignment in one of the churches planned an elaborate sunrise service in connection with the local church. All the previous Saturday they had been busy sweeping a clearing on the campus and outlining with whitewash a map on the ground which included the countries from northwest China to Jerusalem. They had not collaborated with Mark about the program before he went away but had felt that God wanted them to give a missionary slant to the entire sunrise service. Individual students had looked up the population, area in square miles, number of Christians, and hindrances to the gospel in each country.

As Easter morning began to dawn, the Christians heard a bleak, cold wind blowing and looked outside their homes to see a light snow whirling about on the ground. They wrapped in their warmest clothing and shoes, and those who had them wore fur-lined coats. No one remained home from the service because of inclement weather. A circle formed around the big map on the ground.

Following the singing of Easter hymns, the program proceeded. One student after another paced out the area on the map for the country that he represented, stated the dire spiritual needs of that land, and then invited the listeners to come and stand on the country to which they felt God was leading them. At the close of the service two or more young people were standing on each of these unevangelized countries and, many of them with tears, were praying for God's guidance for themselves or for others to go and claim these territories for Christ. Those of us present would never forget that memorable Easter sunrise service. God had spoken to many hearts. People forgot the cold wind and snow and tarried around the outline map, reluctant to leave the presence of the Lord.

"God has called me to work in Afghanistan." "God wants me to go to Sinkiang." "God has called me to work in Tsinghai." Students greeted Mark as he returned to the campus at the close of the Easter weekend.

Mark called a meeting of all students and faculty members Monday evening. He reported how God had called him to open work in central Asia and how he had been puzzled about where he could possibly find workers to go to these fields and funds to support them. "But while God was speaking to me as I meditated by the riverside, He has at the same time called individual workers for each of these nations of central Asia."

One after another of the students, with deep emotion, told of God's call to them in the Easter sunrise service. Earnest prayer followed the testimonies and all agreed that those interested should meet once a week to pray for funds, for personnel, for equipment, and for guidance in entering upon this great work. At one of the subsequent meetings they decided to call themselves the Back-to-Jerusalem Evangelistic Band.

The nearest territory in their travels westward was Kansu and then Sinkiang. The latter was sometimes controlled by China and sometimes contested by

Russia. There were frequent border disputes between these two countries as they vied for possession of this mineral rich region.

At that time China was in control and had appointed a Muslim as governor. He was intensely anti-Christian and refused to allow Christian preachers even to enter the area. The students and faculty began to pray that God would, in His own way, open the door to Sinkiang.

A short time after this special prayer meeting, as Mark was reading the daily newspaper his eyes hit upon a tiny news item which attracted his attention: "Muslim Governor of Sinkiang replaced by General Chang Chin Chiang." His heart almost leaped to his mouth. The new governor was an earnest Christian who had distributed tens of thousands of New Testaments to Chinese soldiers. He was known throughout the whole country as an ardent Christian. What a time of praise the Band had as this news item, a direct answer to their prayers, was announced!

Money began to pour in to them from unexpected Chinese sources. Wash basins, woolen blankets, quilts were donated to them. With each gift the Band knew that this was a confirmation of God's approval and provision for the venture.

One young man in the Northwest Bible Institute knew that God was leading him to go to one of the nations of central Asia, but was not sure which one. He prayed daily that God would make it clear. Then for two successive nights he had the same dream. He saw a bright cloud in the sky on which was written the two Chinese characters for Mecca. The first time he dreamed it, he saw no meaning to it. But after the second dream he began to ask, "What is Mecca?"

"Mecca!" a teacher replied. "Mecca is the holy city of the Muslims. It is located in Arabia. Every true Muslim hopes that he can make at least one journey to the holy city, Mecca, before he dies."

"Now I understand," replied the student. "This is God showing where my future field of labor is to be. I must begin to make a thorough study of the Muslim religion."

He bought Muslim books and set about learning all he could about Muslim beliefs and customs. He even changed his given name to Mecca.

Members of the Band were increasingly convinced that the time had come to begin to send out workers. Funds and equipment were on hand. The first group of three men and five women started out on the long trek. They traveled by bus and by oxcart.

When they reached the panhandle of China's northwest province, Kansu, it was necessary for them to purchase camels for use in crossing the southwestern part of the Gobi Desert in order to reach Sinkiang. They set out early in the spring assured that desert travel would be completed before the winter set in. No one dared venture across the desert during the wintertime with its snows and sub-zero weather. They had taken every precaution that their passports and papers were in order. Week after week they endured the scorching summer sun on the sand and the hot, burning winds. Joyfully they reached the border of Sinkiang.

"You must return to Kansu," said the official. "You lack one important signature on each permit. It will be necessary to return to Lanchow the capital of Kansu to get it."

No urging or persuading would convince the responsible official to allow them to enter Sinkiang. Nor would he allow one person to return for signatures while the others waited at the borders. There was nothing for the group to do but mount their camels and return to Lanchow. They realized that it would be necessary for them to hurry across the desert lest winter overtake them.

Weeks later heavy-hearted young people arrived back at Northwest Bible Institute. They would not be able to set out again for Sinkiang until the following spring. While the winter snows lay on the ground, they obtained the necessary signatures and the next spring again crossed the desert on camels, en route to their desired countries. This time they were admitted to Sinkiang without difficulty.

Because of the high percentage of Muslims living in the territory, persecutions broke out as soon as the young people began to evangelize. Mark led a second party of recruits to Sinkiang in a jeep which had been donated to the Band by a Chinese Christian who desired to expedite their travel. Muslim leaders were unhappy that Christians were permitted to enter the area and disseminate their teachings among the inhabitants.

But when they saw the second contingent arrive in a jeep, they thought that this must be the beginning of a Christian invasion of central Asia, and began to incite mobs to attack the Christian workers or any of the populace who expressed a desire to believe in Christ. The lives of the workers were threatened. A mob seized the jeep, set fire to it, and pushed it over a steep cliff. But this did not discourage the band of young workers, who still retained confidence in God. They had been called and led of God, and no hardship could keep them from carrying on His work.

Gradually some of the Band pushed farther and farther into central Asia on toward Jerusalem. One worker reached the borders of Afghanistan and learned that language preparatory to entering the country. Others reached the borders of Pakistan, where ordinarily it had been impossible for Western missionaries to gain admittance. Mecca married a young woman of the team and together they labored among Muslims, gradually proceeding toward Arabia.

At this point political changes in China interrupted the work of the Band. The Bamboo Princess died on the trek. All but one of the group returned to China. Mark himself was obliged to take up secular employment and turned to watch repairing.

When the Cultural Revolution finally ended and freedom of worship was once again restored in China, Mark was invited to preach the first sermon in the reopened church in the city where he and his family now live.

Chapter Ten

BARNABAS

PRINCIPAL OF CHRISTIAN REFUGEE SCHOOL

"A sword for my New. Year's present!" exclaimed five-year-old Barnabas (People's Comforter) as he brandished his wooden sword. "You couldn't have bought me anything I would like better. Look at the yellow, red, and green colors! Ma, I'm going to be a soldier when I become a man."

"A soldier!" remonstrated his mother. "We do not plan for you to be a soldier. Next year we plan to invite a teacher to come to our home to teach you. You will become either a doctor, a lawyer, or a teacher when you grow up. No son of ours will be a soldier. Soldiers are not respected in our country. Only those who can't find other work become soldiers."

Barnabas ended the argument by running off to find some neighbor children to whom he could show his new sword.

Just as his mother had promised, a year later the best teacher from the whole area appeared at their gate to begin instructing Barnabas. Day after day teacher and pupil sat opposite each other at the table, one drinking tea, and the other droning out Chinese proverbs from the Classics. Barnabas also learned how to make his own ink and to write Chinese characters with a brush.

"I don't like to learn these proverbs," complained Barnabas to his parents weeks later. "It isn't fun. Do I have to study all the time? A lot of the neighbor boys have fun all day long while I have to work over my books. May I quit?"

"No, you may not quit studying," replied his father. "Other boys do not have enough money to invite a teacher to their home. We expect you to grow up to be a gentleman and to be able to make an easy living for yourself and your family. In a few years you will thank us for giving you a good education."

Not wanting to disappoint his parents, Barnabas continued his daily routine.

When Barnabas was twelve years old, the government took control of the education of the whole country and established a public school system which included both boys and girls. The Chinese Classics were replaced by modern textbooks like those used in Western nations. Though drastic social changes take root slowly, Barnabas's parents fell in line with changing custom and sent all of their children to public school. Finding the new curriculum interesting, Barnabas threw himself into his studies with enthusiasm. The three years of junior high school flew by, and he was ready for graduation.

"What can I do next year?" he asked his father toward the close of the school year. "I would like to go on to high school and after that to college. What do you think of that, Father? I would like to get all the modern education that I can."

"We will have to see if we can rent a place for you to stay in the city where the high school is located," replied his father. "We have friends there. I will go into the city soon and see if they will let you rent a room with them. I want to give you the best education possible."

It was arranged for Barnabas to room and board with friends of the family in the provincial capital of Hopei. Because of the distance from home, he was able to return home only during the long winter and summer vacations.

Barnabas was an alert pupil, usually standing at the top of his class. After graduation from high school he entered an agricultural college. Because he enjoyed studying and was also a voracious reader, he failed to get the physical exercise that he needed. There still remained in the back of his mind the old idea that the scholar never runs, never exerts himself until he perspires, and never soils his hands or his silk clothing. The hollow chest and long fingernails announce to everyone whom he meets that he is a highly respected scholar. Even during the transitional period from the ancient to the modern system of education, many young men did not become involved in sports or physical exertion.

In Barnabas's final year in college, his parents were fortunate to find a bride for him who had received a junior high school education. They were married at New Year. The bride remained with his parents while he went back to finish school.

After Barnabas was graduated from college, he began to look for some place where he could pursue further education. He had tasted modern education and wanted more. He heard of a keen, patriotic young man fired with the idea that China should no longer be divided into areas ruled by warlords but should become a unified nation with a central government. This young man, General Chiang Kai-shek, was now head of the Hwang Poo Military Academy in South China, which he patterned after America's West Point Military Academy. Graduates from this school, General Chiang hoped, would organize a modern army which would use modern tactics and equipment.

Barnabas was admitted to one of the earliest classes of Hwang Poo Military Academy. Again he threw himself into his studies with all of his energies.

He found that the commandant of the Academy had an infectious love for his country which fired his students with the same fervor and zeal that he himself had. Among other courses, they studied the writings of Dr. Sun Yat-sen, father of the country, who also was inspired with a vision of a unified China, free from foreign concessions and special privileges.

Graduates from the Academy would become leaders in the national movement which would unify and reorganize the whole nation. Barnabas and his classmates were optimistic for the future of their country. They applied themselves to their lessons and daily discussed what part they would play in the revolution which must take place in China. Their commandant inspired them to attempt great things for their country.

Upon graduation from the Academy, Barnabas was made an officer in the national army. He and his classmates began immediately to train a modern army. No sacrifice was too great for them to endure to accomplish their purpose. Russian advisers were brought into the country to help modernize the army and the thinking of those under them. Hopes seemed nearer fruition each day as more and more educated young men enlisted in the army. No longer was the army composed of illiterate men; it had the cream of the educated youth.

"This army is much different from the old style of army," said Barnabas as he looked out over his neatly-uniformed, well-educated troops. "With men like these we will transform our nation until it stands alongside the great powers of the world. It is an honor to be a part of such an army."

But Barnabas soon found that he was physically unable to continue his duties. Weariness overcame him, accompanied by extreme weakness. Daily he forced himself to carry out his work. At last he was forced to ask permission to go home and recuperate.

"General, may I have several months' leave of absence?" he asked his superior officer. "I seem to be weary all the time and have not the strength to perform the tasks assigned to me. I regret that it is necessary for me to make this request."

"Yes," came the reply. "I have been noticing how thin you have become. Go home to your native Hopei and see if the good air there helps you to recuperate. Take a thorough rest and then come back and help us carry out the revolution."

Emaciated and worn, he finally reached home. When his parents, his wife, and his children saw him, they were shocked at his weakened condition. They bought quantities of incense and paper money to offer to the idols in his behalf. They supported his weak body as daily he worshiped the ancestors and idols in the town temple and also at the shrine in their home. They prepared chicken, fish, pork, fresh fruits, and other delicacies in the most savory manner, offered them first to the idols and then gave them to the sick man to eat. Nothing seemed to produce results.

He continued to waste away until it was impossible for him to leave his bed. Though medicines were prescribed and taken regularly in large doses, he still continued to become thinner and weaker. Both he and his family had exhausted everything they had heard of that might be effective, but all ended in failure.

Barnabas had never attended a Christian church. At one point he had come under the influence of Feng Yu-hsiang, the "Christian General." He knew that there were missionaries in his country teaching about a man named Jesus. But, to him, Jesus was only a "holy man" from the West. Why should he worship Him? China had her own holy men. It was not necessary for him to worship a holy man belonging to the foreigners. Jesus was a man just like Confucius and Mencius of his own country. Consequently, Barnabas had never gone to church to hear about Jesus and His teachings. His esteemed commandant at the Military Academy was a Buddhist who worshiped the idols, and that religion was good enough for him, too.

During the hot summer months as his health continued to fail, he found that the noise of people talking wearied him. Children coming and going or playing near him set his nerves tingling until he wanted to cry out in despair. Even lying on the bed indoors made him feel so confined that he thought he would lose his mind.

"Get me a bamboo cot and carry me out to the back yard away from everybody and everything," he said to his parents one day when they came to feed him some nourishing broth. "The bamboo trees will provide plenty of shade and I can be quiet there away from everyone."

They bought a simple bamboo cot, placed it beside his bed, and using every precaution not to hurt him, lifted his emaciated body onto it. Slowly and tenderly, they carried him to the back of the lot where he would be secluded among the bamboos and other shrubbery. Tears filled his mother's eyes as she walked back to the house. She felt sure that her son would never return to the house alive. She stopped before the family shrine and offered more incense to the idols and to the ancestors. Then she carried him some bland chicken soup, hoping thereby to give him new strength. He had been too weak for weeks to worship the idols, but his wife and members of his family substituted for him.

When his mother brought him chicken soup and other delicacies, he turned away from them after merely sampling them. He preferred not to be bothered with food. He was too weak to feed himself, and nothing he ate seemed to have any flavor anyway. He enjoyed the gentle sighing of the wind in the slender branches of the graceful bamboo that swayed over his head. With his eyes closed most of the time he lay and listened to their gentle sighing sound. Members of his family wondered how he could continue to live.

Barnabas began to think serious thoughts. "Can there be a God somewhere? Where did the world come from? Where did man come from? Who keeps the world and the universe revolving without collision? China has Confucius, Mencius, and Lao Tzu. The Western world has Jesus, George Washington, and Lincoln, but what nation knows about a God?"

His mother would tiptoe out to the edge of the trees frequently to see if her son was still alive. She could not understand how he could linger on so many days. She had made a new white cotton suit and put it on him so that he would be ready for burial.

One day as he lay there quietly thinking about a God who could control the universe, he was startled by a voice that seemed to come from the sky, "Jesus is God. He is not a man. Worship Him."

Startled, he looked around to see who was talking to him. There was no one in sight. He closed his eyes and began to think of the words he had heard.

"Jesus is God. He is not a man. Worship Him." Again came the loud voice even clearer than the first time.

He knew now that someone was talking to him. He said aloud, "There is a God; He is speaking to me! He is telling me to worship Jesus. He is informing me that Jesus is God and not just a holy man."

Realizing that he was lying in the presence of the God of the universe, he struggled to get out of the bed. With superhuman effort he sat up and then stood to his feet. No one happened to be near him at the time. Under the swaying bamboos, with great effort, he knelt on the ground.

"Jesus is God. Jesus is God," he sobbed. "Jesus is not a man. I have never worshiped Him. Jesus, forgive my sins! I have never worshiped You. I have worshiped only man. I have never worshiped God. Please forgive me."

Tears flowed freely over his emaciated face. But as he prayed, the tears ceased. Joy came to his heart. Peace such as he had never known filled his heart.

With great exertion he arose from his knees and began to walk slowly toward his home. He met his mother coming out of the house to see how he was. Startled by his sunken eyes, fleshless face and body, and the loose-fitting white burial garment, she screamed, "My son! You will die! You will die! Why did you leave your bed?"

"Jesus is God," he said excitedly. "He is not a man. Buddha is a man. He is not God."

His mother, fearing he had lost his reason, started to run to the house.

"Jesus is God, Mother. He is not a man," he kept saying fervently as he continued to walk slowly toward the house. "Jesus has given me peace, Jesus will make me well. From today on we must worship Jesus. We must not worship Buddha or any other idols. They were men. They are not God. Let us take them all down. They cannot give peace. They were men."

His frightened mother saw him begin to throw the incense and other articles of worship out into the courtyard. Though she tried to restrain him, he continued. At first she thought he was mentally deranged, but when she saw his strength and realized that his words were not irrational, she began to comprehend that something supernatural had taken place.

Barnabas's strength returned rapidly as he began to

eat and digest food. At his request, the family found a
Christian church in the city whose pastor came to visit
them. He brought them a Bible and told them more
clearly the way of salvation. Barnabas's wife and both
his parents, turning to the Lord, became earnest
Christians. Afterward it was a common sight to see all
of them walking together to the Christian church.
Barnabas read the Bible to them daily. As God opened
the Scriptures to him in a remarkable way, he began
to win his friends to Christ.

Meantime the revolution that would unify China
continued to progress from south to north. Generalissimo Chiang Kai-shek with his Russian advisers was
successful in overthrowing the warlords who had been
bleeding the country of taxes and resources. In village
after village they had robbed and killed landowners.
The Russians advised that the best way to put
communism into practice was to clear the land of all
occupants, divide it up equally and begin with a clear
slate. The advancing army slaughtered all the people
of the area who could not escape and stacked their
corpses into mounds. They let them lie in the sun until
the crows and buzzards had eaten all the flesh from
their bones and then burned as many of the bones as
possible.

As the Generalissimo saw what his advisers were
doing, he realized that this was not what China
needed. This policy would never unify China.
Consequently, he broke with the Russian advisers. But
they were unwilling to leave the country. They
withdrew from the Generalissimo, taking away with
them a large group of young officers and men who
still felt that communism would bring unity to the
land.

While the Northern Expedition was being success-
fully carried forward, Generalissimo Chiang noticed
that though many missionaries had been advised to

leave the war zone, they had not done so. They remained at their posts and kept their hospitals open for the treatment of the sick and wounded. In spite of the fact that his soldiers had desecrated many missionaries' residences and some of the churches, the missionaries did not retaliate, but cared for the wounded and sick among his troops as though they were friends and not enemies. He began to wonder why they could do this. His mother-in-law, Mrs. Song, was an earnest Christian who prayed daily that he would turn to Christ. Missionaries, ordered to the coast by their governments because of the war, also spent days in fasting and prayer not only for the country but also for the leader of the troops, who was in reality the leader of the nation.

One day the newspapers of the country blazoned the headlines, "GENERAL CHIANG KAI-SHEK BECOMES A CHRISTIAN AND IS BAPTIZED." From that day on the attitude of his troops toward the church and the missionaries was reversed.

Meanwhile Barnabas began to travel widely, ministering in many places and among different denominational groups. He met the Reverend E. P. Ashcraft, pioneer Free Methodist missionary in China, and through his fellowship and teaching came into the experience of entire sanctification.

He was impressed when he saw many missionaries and Chinese pastors giving their time each day to feed multitudes of refugees who had fled from Japanese-occupied territory to a camp in Free China. Thousands of tons of grain were stored there to be dispensed to the hungry who had left home and had no way to make a livelihood. Men, women, and children were crowded together in barracks or in deserted homes in the city. Every morning and evening, services were conducted for them with the hope that many would be won to Christ. Teachers were employed for a refugee school that was set up by the churches. Most of the missionaries who were carrying on this humanitarian work were elderly people. Barnabas observed that they were worn out, following many months of strenuous labor, and that they needed a change. Missionary Ashcraft invited Barnabas to join the team and head up the work of relief and education among the refugees. This was a place where a scrupulously honest administrator was needed. He accepted.

Under his systematic, conscientious direction, the work went forward smoothly. Yet everyone was under constant tension, because the refugee camp was separated from the Japanese armies by only the Yellow River. The government had opened the dikes diverting the river from its northeasterly course to a southeasterly course. Changing the course of the river had held up the Japanese military advance for two years, forcing the enemy to plan new strategy for getting their heavy armored equipment and their armies across the Yellow River.

"The Japanese are planning to cross the Yellow River far west of our city," announced an intelligence officer one morning to Barnabas. "Your refugee school is no longer safe in this area. They are mobilizing heavy concentrations of troops and boats. You will have to plan to escape at once."

"West of here!" exclaimed Barnabas. "Have they cut the railroad? We will have to walk three days to reach the railroad and then get onto trains to take us farther west."

"You must not wait," replied the officer. "Call the school together at once and have each pupil pack his bedding and what possessions he can carry on his back. There is no time for delay."

Barnabas called his teachers together and asked them to organize their classes into marching bands. Classes were dismissed and students prepared for early departure. Older students who could travel faster set off right after lunch for the three-day trek to the railroad. A few of the earliest groups were successful in boarding a train which took them westward. But before the others got there, Japanese planes bombed and cut the railroad. Now the only way of escape was through a circuitous route overland through mountain trails. Nine hundred students, teachers and families quickly changed the course of their flight. Miss Edith Jones, a veteran missionary who was past retirement age, traveled with the smaller children on the long trek.

During the day the large body of fleeing refugees often became the target for Japanese bombing and strafing attacks. Miraculously no one was killed. How true God's promise was. "A thousand may fall at your side, ten thousand at your right hand, but it will not come near you. . . . For he will command his angels concerning you to guard you in all your ways" (Psalm 91:7, 11).

At night they crowded together on the floor or in the courtyards of Chinese inns. With some traveling faster and some slower, they were able to find a place for all to sleep at night.

Two adults were sent ahead to the far northwest to try to find quarters for the whole group where they could keep the school intact. God had years before made provision for them. A wealthy farmer with only a few members in his family had built large numbers of buildings in his courtyard where he hoped to open a school some day. He could occupy only a small portion of the rooms. When Barnabas approached him to allow this Christian school to occupy his premises, he readily granted permission. Though he refused other groups in the past, now he did all in his power to make ready for the refugee students.

When nine hundred footsore, weary people arrived

at their destination, they found the rooms were already cleaned and ready, and hot food for them was steaming in the kettles. Chinese and American relief organizations supplied the school with food for the duration of the war.

Classes were conducted in an orderly manner under their principal, Barnabas. Morning and evening prayers were held daily. Sunday services were conducted by faculty members or by advanced students from nearby Northwest Bible Institute. Evangelistic services were also conducted twice a year. Many of the young people sought and found the Lord and some of them, after graduation, entered the ministry.

One glorious day in August, 1945, a messenger came riding a bicycle into the schoolyard and shouting, "The war is ended. Japan has surrendered! You will all soon be able to go back home! The war is over!"

Great joy filled the hearts of these refugees as they thought of being reunited with their families. Many, though, had no idea where their families had gone. When the fighting had neared their homes, families had become frightened and had run in different directions to find some place to escape the fighting. Now that the war was ended, millions of displaced persons did not know whether they would find anyone living in the old home if they returned. Some had established new homes and new businesses in west China and chose to remain in the new locality.

Barnabas and his board of directors spent many hours deliberating over what they should do about the refugee school. Since a difficult reconstruction period faced the entire nation, they knew that it would be a long time until the government would be able to provide schools for all of the young people who would want to attend. Their final decision was that they would keep the school intact and return to Honan. The principal and faculty would return with them, and if the parents had returned home, their children could leave the school and live with the parents. Those who could not find their parents could remain at the school until they finished high school.

It was a big undertaking to move the entire school back to its original location, but it was done with meticulous planning. Barnabas, with his military training, knew just how to plan for transportation, food, and quarters for the large group. Advance men had been sent ahead to provide living quarters for the students and teachers. All had become accustomed to refugee life and found it easy to proceed with classes.

After the fall of the Nationalist government it was again necessary for leaders of the refugee school to make far-reaching decisions. Many of the children in the school had not yet established contact with their parents. Many others preferred to remain in the refugee school because the government schools in most places were not yet functioning. Barnabas and most of the faculty members decided to remain with the refugee school under the new government.

No one was exempt from communist examinations and purgings. People's courts were set up. Accusation meetings were held in all towns. This was an opportunity for people who had old hatreds and grudges to get even with their enemies. When kangaroo courts were set up, people were called upon to bring accusations against those who were put up for trial. These consisted of landowners, officials, or business people. Propagandists had already promised that if these "capitalists" were accused, their possessions would be divided equally among everyone. All sorts of false accusations were made. Children were urged by the communists to accuse their parents even when they knew it would lead to the assassination of their parents. Some parents accused children to their death. Pupils accused teachers. Neighbors accused neighbors. Everyone had to do some accusing.

Barnabas was not exempt. As soon as the communist troops entered the city, they sought out the refugee school. They asked where the principal got so much money to operate this large school. They would not believe that International Relief was providing the funds for such a large operation. He was accused of dishonesty in the handling of funds. Barnabas became a special target.

"Renounce your Christianity and we will let you go," shouted his accusers.

"No," Barnabas replied. "I can never, never renounce Christ. If necessary I will die first."

"Don't be an idiot," they screamed. "Renounce Christ, and you will have your freedom."

"No," answered Barnabas. "Christ is my best friend. I cannot turn my back on Him. He has cleansed my heart and will take me home to heaven if I am faithful to Him."

"Have your way," they shouted. "Take what you get."

They disbanded the school. Some of the students were able to make their escape to Hong Kong, but most of them remained. Barnabas was thrown into prison to brainwash him of his Christianity, which was the main charge against him. But Christ meant too much to Barnabas for him to deny his Lord. Though all sorts of punishments and tortures were used while he was in prison, he steadfastly refused to renounce Christ. His oldest daughter, by that time in high school, was permitted to visit her father in prison several times and take him some food and clean clothing.

Then the last time she went to see him, a guard

shouted at her, "What do you want? Why do you keep coming here? Get out of here at once and never let us see your face again!"

"I have brought food and clean clothes for my father," she remonstrated.

"Don't argue with me!" he shouted. "Get out of here at once. Don't ever come back or you'll get it, too. Christians are enemies of the people. Get out!" He started toward her with a fixed bayonet. She slipped away.

It was not until after the overthrow of the Gang of Four that Barnabas was finally released and his civil liberty restored. Though he had suffered much during his prison experience, today he is fearlessly preaching the Word and witnessing of Jesus' power to save.

Chapter Eleven

JULIA

THE TRAGEDY OF AN UNBELIEVING SPOUSE

"Commencement just a few months away! I can't believe it," exclaimed Jane, a high school senior, as she pushed into a dormitory room full of talkative girls. "Mary, what do you plan to do when you finish school? I suppose something exciting where you'll make a lot of money."

"You guessed it," replied Mary. "I expect to operate a night club seven days a week. They say there is a lot of money in that and a lot of good times."

"Priscilla, what are your plans for the future?" continued Jane. "I suppose your parents have your life all mapped out for you."

"My parents have been generous with me," answered Priscilla. "I owe my entire education to them. They have mortgaged our farm so that I could go to high school. I plan to return home and teach in a Christian elementary school operated by my home church. In that way I can help my parents pay off the mortgage and can also help in the local church."

"You are a goodie-goodie," broke in Julia. "We would all expect you to do something like that. My parents have also denied themselves a lot of things so that I can attend school here, but I don't see why I have to let them run my life for me. I expect to find a school far away from home where I can teach and earn a lot of money. I like pretty clothes and lots of fun. I'll be glad when I can get away from where they try to force religion on us. I had the same thing all the years that I lived at home. I'll be glad when I can be on my own and do as I please. My parents spend a lot of time every day praying that I will follow their Christian pattern of life, but I intend to plan my own future."

The conversation continued along this line until all had expressed their ideas of how they would spend their future.

The school was certainly operated as a Christian school, but many of the students who attended were not Christians. The government had not yet opened many high schools for girls. Since the Christian church had taken the lead in making provision for the education of both boys and girls, many young people flocked to the Christian schools where they could get a good education at reduced rates, but many of these young people did not intend to accept Christian beliefs.

Julia's father, a postal employee, was an earnest Christian, who had committed her to the Lord in early infancy, and was now working hard to meet the expense of her education. Julia, on the other hand, had a special affinity for those young people who had no interest in Christianity. As Julia heard the other girls talk about their secular plans when they finished school, she, too, began to plan for a life where she could command a high salary and eventually set up a wealthy home from which God was excluded. But daily at home, her parents prayed that God would bring some circumstances into her life that would wean her away from the things of the world.

One morning during the daily chapel service, it was announced that because Dr. John Sung, a very special speaker, would visit the school a month later, there would be no classes for a week but all students would be required to attend daily services. Loud applause followed the announcement. The students were all excited as they walked from the auditorium to their classes.

"Dr. John Sung?" one asked. "Who is he? Why did so many students clap their hands when they heard that he is coming here for a week of meetings?"

"You must have read about him in the newspapers," replied a Christian student. "He is a native-born son of China. He is a great scholar. He studied in America, where he graduated with honors. He has a doctor of philosophy degree from Ohio State University. There they granted him highest honors by giving him a gold key."

"Is he coming here to lecture on chemistry?" asked another.

"No. Didn't you hear them announce that he is coming here to preach to us?" said another.

"Oh, no," groaned the first student. "Not another preacher! Haven't we had enough preaching here this year?"

"But this man is different," protested the Christian student. "Dr. John Sung's father was a Methodist preacher for many years in south China. John decided that he would never be a preacher. He would major in chemistry, return to China to do research in chemistry and amass a fortune with which he could support his father in his old age and also educate his younger brothers and sisters."

"Then why is he coming here to preach?" asked a skeptic. "I would rather hear him talk about all the chemistry he learned in America."

"After he attended Ohio State University," continued the Christian, "he became a real Christian. He studied his Bible daily and began to do personal work among students in New York. While he traveled on the ship back to China, one night as he was walking around on the deck, God began to talk to him and asked him to return to China as a preacher. At first he refused because he felt that his father, having given his entire life as a poor preacher, had made sufficient sacrifice for the work of the Lord. But as he paced the deck until almost daybreak, God continued to talk to him and show him that China needed the gospel more than it needed chemistry research. As God continued to press His claims, John Sung raised both hands toward heaven and exclaimed there in the moonlight, 'O Lord, here is my life! Take it and use it. Who am I that I dare to contend with the Almighty who gave His life to save my soul? If God will use me, I will preach the gospel no matter what it costs me.'

"His mind was made up. So he would not be tempted to turn from this commitment, he went down to his cabin, removed from his trunk his diploma from Ohio State University and his gold key, returned to the deck, and threw them into the Pacific Ocean.

" 'From today forward, I want only the honors that come from God,' he exclaimed, 'now no earthly power can pull me back.' "

"He was really a fool to do such a thing," shouted one of the listeners. "If I had a diploma from an American university and a gold key in chemistry, I would use them to make money. China needs chemists."

"There is more than one standard of success," replied the Christian student. "As God looks at Dr. Sung, he is having great success. Wherever he goes, large crowds attend his meetings. In most cities no church is large enough to hold the crowds that attend. Thousands have already been won to Christ through him. And Dr. Sung is still a young man. You will not be disappointed when you hear him preach."

"I'd say he is a nut," continued the skeptic. "I'll

hide my textbook in my Bible when I go to his services and study instead of listening to a man who is not all there."

For a whole month the students talked excitedly of this famous Chinese scholar who was soon to visit their school. Julia was among the many who anticipated hearing him but had no intention of becoming a Christian. She would soon be out of school and would be entering upon her life's career. Already she had been accepted for a teaching position in a county that was pushing modern education and was choosing only the most promising young people for its schools.

All was excitement in the town the day John Sung arrived. The girls and the hundreds from the city who attended the meetings were disappointed to find that the preacher was a short, wiry man with a most unattractive face, overhung by a crop of stubborn hair. But they were not disappointed when they heard him preach. He chose Bible stories which he acted out before their very eyes. He ran back and forth across the platform, made all sorts of grimaces as he talked, drew his face into contortions, waved his arms for emphasis until, at the close of each message, his clothing was wet with perspiration. He put every ounce of his energy into each sermon. Following each message, crowds rushed to the front of the church to pray for forgiveness.

Students who had agreed beforehand that they would never respond to his preaching rushed to the front of the church and repented. During the first two days, Julia attended every meeting, but tried to steel her heart against Dr. Sung's invitation to let Jesus save her. But conviction deepened and the third day she found herself going forward with many others to seek the Lord. As she yielded her life to Christ, He came into her heart and her whole being was filled with the joy of the Lord. Short, graceful Julia, after she found the Lord, skipped for joy as she went singing about the school. Before the meetings with Dr. Sung had closed, she had answered God's call to His service. Her parents' joy knew no bounds when they received her letter reporting what God had done for her and how she had committed her life to His service. They were more interested in her serving the Lord than they were in her accumulating wealth.

In early autumn she left home to take her first teaching position. That county offered an award, at the end of the first semester, for the one whom they would choose as the model teacher of the county. When she began teaching, Julia applied the most modern methods in her classroom. Her enthusiasm was infectious to her students and they did their best work. At the end of the first semester, she was delighted when she received the model teacher's award. All of her associates were happy for her, especially Mr. S., who had been her silent admirer all of the year. He was a staunch Buddhist, tall, handsome, and wealthy. Many of the single women teachers admired him, but his eyes were only for Julia. He sought opportunities to be with her. She, seeing his many good qualifications, liked him. But the big drawback lay in the fact that he was not a Christian. Night after night she tossed on her bed wondering what she should do. Did not Paul remind early Christians, "Do not be yoked together with unbelievers. For what do righteousness and wickedness have in common?"

One time when she went home for a holiday, he accompanied her so that her parents might meet him. While there he told them that he would like to marry Julia. Though they recognized his talents, both of her parents objected to the marriage.

Mr. S. then used the timeworn argument of the non-Christian, "I do not understand Christianity, but I would like to. If you will allow us to keep company, Julia can teach me how to become a Christian."

The parents knew the dangers of this course and still flatly refused. Inexperienced Julia, however, thought that he sounded reasonable and continued to meet with him frequently after school.

When she took him home the second time for her parents to get better acquainted with him, he said, "Just let us get married and then Julia can help me in our own home to become a Christian."

When her parents still refused, Julia made her own decision. She would marry him. It would be her work for God to lead him and his family to the Lord.

Contrary to her parents' wishes, she married him. According to Chinese custom, the ceremony is performed in the home of the husband. But he knew that she would not consent to a traditional Chinese wedding at which they would have to worship idols and ancestors, so they were married before the school year closed in a Christian church in the town where they taught. As soon as they were married, he lost all interest in Christianity. When Julia tried to explain it to him, he replied, "Why not be modern? Christianity is the religion of capitalism. Young people today are embracing Marxism. That is the philosophy of the future. Only communism can save our country." Too shocked to reply, Julia refused to accept his philosophy.

When they went to his home at the close of the school term, Julia was astonished to see how idolatrous his whole family was. Both parents were illiterate and began each day burning incense at the family shrine to both idols and ancestors. Each member of the family was expected to participate in worship in the home every morning and also to go to the temples at stated times each year to worship the idols there. Julia refused to have any part in idolatrous worship. While they worshiped the idols, she took the time to kneel in prayer to God. For this reason her mother-in-law despised her. Because Julia was expecting her first child, she did not return to her teaching that fall, but remained in her husband's home and helped with the never-ending work in the house or in the fields. She made countless efforts to introduce the subject of Christianity to different members of her husband's family but was repulsed by each one.

Even though her first child was a boy, which should have brought great joy, her mother-in-law and the other members of the family still hated her. When her husband tried to be kind to her, the others mocked him and showed their dislike of her even more. There was no excitement in the home when a girl was born to her the following summer. Other sons in the home had children who joined in the worship of the idols and ancestors. Julia was so constantly held up to ridicule that her husband decided that he should leave home. He told the family, "My country needs me. World War II is raging and I want to do what I can to drive out the Japanese."

It would have been a relief to Julia to go with him, but she was expecting her third child, and how could she care for three children away from home? Where would the funds come from? She longed to return to her own family, but Chinese custom forbade it. When a girl is married, she must remain in her husband's home and do her share of the work. With her husband away, Julia's life was made even more miserable. Each member of his family vied with the others to say unkind things to her. She tried to pray, but it seemed that God did not hear. She had disobeyed Him by marrying a heathen man, and now she was suffering for it. To add to her troubles, when the third child, a son, was born, she became paralyzed from the waist down. She could not leave her bed. The family grudgingly waited on her.

Then came a letter from her husband who was hundreds of miles away. "Come at once to be with me here up north. Do not delay. Come right now." She replied, "I am paralyzed and cannot walk. I cannot possibly come. How can I travel so far alone in war times with three small children?" His reply soon followed, "How long do you expect me to get along without a wife? Come at once in any way that you can. Otherwise I will find a wife here. Leave the children with my mother and come on."

Julia wept as she spread the selfish letter before the Lord. She prayed for God to heal her. Then a neighbor told her of a nearby doctor who had cured several local mothers who had become paralyzed at childbirth. Her mother-in-law invited the doctor. He gave Julia a brew of Chinese herbs which had good results. Gradually the paralysis left her and she was able to move about the house. As soon as she was able to walk out of doors she asked the family for money, and carrying the smallest son in her arms, started on the long journey to find her husband. It was with a breaking heart that she left the two oldest children behind with their heathen grandmother. She knew that as soon as she was gone they would be forced to worship the idols.

Day after day she traveled till she reached Shensi, the southern half of the province in Nationalist hands while the northern half was occupied by communist armies. As Julia inquired for the town where her husband was located, she found that he was in communist territory. She was frightened to proceed and wrote to him asking him to come to her. He came. Among other things he told her that he was thoroughly convinced that communism is the only hope for China and that they should both throw their efforts into advancing the communist cause. When Julia demurred, he issued an ultimatum to her, "Make up your mind in two days. Come with me and promote the cause of communism, or I will report to the marriage bureau that my wife refuses to accompany me here; I will get a divorce and register with another woman. Hurry and make up your mind, for in two days I will return to my work."

Julia's heart was filled with consternation. She debated the matter in her mind day and night. She thought, "He is my husband, the father of my children. If I don't go with him, how will I support the family? On the other hand, I am a Christian. How can a Christian embrace atheistic communism? Can I defy God a second time?"

At the end of the second day, her decision was ready. When her husband asked her what she had decided, she replied, "I cannot give up my faith in the true God for an empty philosophy, however popular it may be. I am sorry I cannot go with you."

He flew into a rage and shouted, "Go your stubborn way if you will! Make a fool of yourself! Follow your Western capitalistic religion! You have had your chance to help your country, but you have refused. Go your way. I am through with you. I will get a wife who is modern in her way of thinking." He rushed out of the door and slammed it, leaving her at the small inn with only a few dollars left in her purse.

As she sat alone with her baby in the inn, tears rushed to her eyes. What should she do? Where could she go? Her money would soon be gone. Where could she find employment where she could take a baby with her?

Julia went to a large city where she found a Christian church not too far away from a small inn where she rented a cheap room. Using the church address, she wrote a letter asking for money from her own brother who had a good position in a distant province. It would be at least a month before his reply could reach her. With strictest economy her money could not possibly last till his reply came.

Day after day with her baby in her arms she searched for work. The whole city was full of refugees who were seeking employment. Every place she went gave the same reply, no. Her heart sank. Had God forsaken her?

As she tramped around the city, she finally found a Christian orphanage that took her on trial for a two-week period. She did her best to please them. For her services she was given her room and board and a small allowance for spending money. At the end of the trial period, they called her to the office and informed her, "Your work has been satisfactory, but we have found a woman to take your place who is not cumbered by children. Please vacate the room for your replacement as soon as possible."

Julia pleaded with them, "Please let me continue to live here until I can find other work." They refused.

Heartsick, she returned to the cheap inn with her precious baby. To add to her distress, her baby began to run a high temperature. She had no money for medicine or doctor's fees. She did her best to care for him, but the temperature continued unabated. As her baby rolled his eyes in delirium, she was almost frantic.

Then one day a woman who lived in the inn told her, "There is a temple not far from here where the idols are especially effective in curing this kind of disease. I have known of several who have gone there to worship, whose children have been cured. Why don't you try it?"

Julia's heart told her that it was wrong, but her emotions urged her to do something to save the life of her child. It could cost only a few cents to buy

185

incense. It was worth trying. She left the baby lying on the bed at the inn, walked to the temple, bought a package of incense and asked an attendant to show her how to use it. In her desperation she prostrated herself before the idols. In her heart she asked them to have pity on her son and heal him. As she walked out of the temple toward the inn, her heart condemned her that she, a Christian, had resorted to deaf idols for help. Her baby was still delirious when she reached the inn. That night as she sat holding him in her arms, he died. How alone she felt! No husband, no child, no money! And she had grieved God by worshiping idols! The next morning the pastor of the Christian church helped her to bury her son.

An enterprising boy who helped support himself and his mother was selling hot steamed bread from door to door every morning. Julia had no money to pay ready cash for the steamed bread, but told him that at the end of the month she would have money and would pay him the total amount due. He was reluctant to believe her because there were many war refugees in the city who were penniless and used dishonest methods to support themselves. Every day he pressed her to pay what she owed and every day she urged him to wait another day or two. She took daily trips to the Christian church to ask them if a letter had come from her brother, but every day they gave her the same negative reply. The preacher and his wife were getting tired of seeing her at their door.

She was deeply depressed. It seemed that God had forsaken her. She had reached the bottom! One day after another fruitless trip to the church, as she was going out of the yard, the gateman called out to her cheerfully, "Did you get your letter? One came for you today." He got it for her. With nervous hands she tore open the long-overdue letter and found a generous check from her brother. After cashing it, she was able to pay the bill for the steamed bread and for her room at the inn. She also had some left for daily expenses.

Several days later she saw a notice in the newspaper that a civil service examination would be held for high school graduates. Julia joined many others who took the tests, and passed. In a few days she was appointed to a responsible position in a government agency, the Bureau of Communications. As her circumstances began to improve, her heart began to turn toward God. It looked as though He was helping her solve her problems after all. Her hunger for God increased and she longed to find someone who would help her in prayer. Her government position took her first to a mushrooming city where there was a tiny church near the west gate.

One Saturday she walked from her office to the church, hoping someone would help her pray. A missionary family was shepherding the church. The missionary wife was in the act of bathing her children in a metal tub in the living room that Saturday afternoon when Julia appeared at their door. Julia told the missionary that she had recently arrived in town and was looking for a Christian church. The missionary, noticing that Julia was educated and refined, went on with bathing the children and replied, "It would be better for you to attend the church in the east end of the city. That church caters to the educated and the better class of people. We have only a few ignorant country women who worship here."

With heavy steps and a heavier heart she retraced her steps, thinking as she walked down the street, "I wonder if God will cast me off forever? Will He never accept me?"

The next morning she went to the big, new church in the east end of town and continued to do so for several Sundays, but the believers were so extreme in their ways of worship that she found nothing to satisfy the hunger of her heart there. Some worshipers, when they prayed, mumbled in what they called an unknown tongue, while others went through strange physical contortions or rolled on the cement floor. Julia became frightened and decided not to return there again.

Just at this time Julia was transferred to a government storage depot out in the country. When Sunday came, she walked three miles in the hot sun to attend the church service. Great was her disappointment when she finally reached the tiny building, to find a notice posted on the door, "Closed for the duration of the war because of bombings."

Tears of disappointment coursed down her cheeks. In her grief she cried aloud as she stood there, "O God, won't I ever be able to get back to You?"

After working for a few weeks in that area, Julia was transferred back to the larger city. On Sunday morning she was so hungry for God that she decided to attend once more the service at the big, new church in the east suburb. As she entered the door of the church, she was surprised to see a woman missionary standing on the platform teaching a hymn to the congregation.

Since, in the wartime, hymnbooks were not available, it was necessary to write the hymns in large Chinese characters on huge sheets of white paper and secure them to a hymn rack on the platform where all could see. My husband and I had just arrived in the city to preach the gospel and had been invited by this church to hold a week of meetings. Julia knew nothing of this but was happy to hear a gospel message. Her eyes turned at once to the song sheet on the platform. Avidly she read the words of the hymn:

All my life long I had panted
    For a draught from some cool spring
That I hoped would quench the burning
    Of the thirst I felt within.

Chorus: Hallelujah! I have found Him
        Whom my soul so long has craved!
     Jesus satisfies my longings;
        Through His blood I now am saved.

Feeding on the husks around me,
    Till my strength was almost gone,
Longed my soul for something better,
    Only still to hunger on.

Poor I was, and sought for riches,
    Something that would satisfy,
But the dust I gathered 'round me
    Only mocked my soul's sad cry.

Well of water, ever springing,
    Bread of life, so rich and free,
Untold wealth that never faileth,
    My Redeemer is to me.

Tears flowed freely as Julia read the lines of the hymn and tears continued to flow through the service as she listened to the gospel message. When an invitation was given for hungry hearts to come forward to seek the Lord, Julia led the way. Kneeling on the cement floor, she wept her way back to God. As God granted His forgiveness, joy filled her.

After her reconciliation she threw herself into the work of the Lord and brought many from her office to services held in our home, where some of them also found the Lord. She taught a class for young people in the Sunday school and also took responsibility for the young people's society.

Julia's two children, being brought up in her husband's home, were a constant burden on her mind. It was impossible for them to travel alone to be with her, and she could not get sufficient time off to go and get them. So she applied to the government to be transferred to an office in a southern province where she could have her children live with her. Her request was granted.

En route to her new office she stopped at her husband's home to get her son and daughter, who were now old enough to attend school. At first her mother-in-law refused to let them go. Her heart was still full of hatred for Julia. After a day or two of reasoning with her, Julia won the mother-in-law's consent. Then Julia set out for her new office, filled with happiness to have her children with her again. She was surprised at the deep inroads that heathen worship had made in their lives. She took them with her to the church services and spent hours in the home teaching them about Jesus. It was not easy to stamp out idolatry from their hearts, but in the end she led them to Christ.

Since her office was responsible for critical storage dumps, workers sometimes had to be transferred to a new area when their location became known to the enemy. God's protection was constantly over her. One time when she was moving to a new location in another province, Julia felt impressed to take a later bus, though it would be a more difficult journey involving night travel. When the bus on which Julia and her children were riding in the afternoon came to a sudden stop, they found a road block. Getting out to investigate, they discovered that the earlier bus had been bombed by enemy planes. Corpses and the dying were scattered all around the destroyed bus. As she helped care for the wounded she was thankful that

God had protected her and her children by having them take a later bus.

Julia never heard from her husband again. She had to assume full responsibility for the support and training of her children. She was earnest in warning other young people against marriage with an unbeliever. Wherever she went, she entered wholeheartedly into the work of the church both with money and with talents.

As Julia looked back on her life she could see that, though at times, she had failed to live for God as she should have, He had been faithful and had brought her back to himself. At times when life was hard and she thought that God had forsaken her, He had always led her until through all of her hardships she could see where God's love was drawing her to himself.

A Bamboo Curtain was drawn across the horizon of Julia and her children, separating them from the outside world. We have heard nothing about her for more than thirty years. But we are certain of one fact — Julia will never again turn her back on her Lord even at the cost of her life.

Chapter Twelve

Mrs. Goong

"I AM AN ATHEIST!"

"Don't waste your time talking to me about your Western God," exclaimed Mrs. Goong to a Chinese medical doctor. "I am an atheist. I don't believe in any god, either Chinese or Western. If there were a god anywhere, the world would not be in the terrible condition in which we now find it. It is because of the devastation, corruption, and dishonesty I see all around me that I am in the physical condition that you see me now. Why do you think I have come to you every day to buy some of your cow's milk? It is because I am on the verge of a complete physical collapse and am drinking milk to strengthen me against it."

"But," replied Dr. Chou, "I know that there is a God. I talk to Him every day and He gives me inward peace and comfort. A few years ago I was as disturbed as you now are. One day a Christian friend visited me, told me of Jesus, and helped me to pray to Him. I had so lost confidence in mankind that I had reached the verge of despair. But as I prayed and confessed my own wrongdoings, Jesus heard me and forgave my sins. He came into my heart and brought me peace. Day by day since then I pray to Him and He gives me the comfort and security that I need."

"It is easy for you to talk because you do not have the problems that I have. Let me tell you some of my troubles. When the Japanese armies approached our city in 1938, our whole family was comfortably settled in the heart of this big city. My husband was a successful businessman. We owned a big store and had a large, comfortable home adjoining it. My father-in-law helped in the business. I taught in the local college. Our three children were happy in school. When enemy bombs rained down on our city, we became so alarmed and confused that all of us ran in different directions in order to save our lives. Only my father-in-law remained at home to try to keep the store going.

One day a Japanese bomb destroyed our store together with the home and killed my father-in-law. My husband and I had run together on foot to try to find some place to hide. Suddenly Japanese planes appeared overhead and sprayed the fleeing refugees with bullets. My husband was hit and in great agony died there by my side in the field. I sat beside his silent body and wailed out my grief alone. Fleeing crowds rushed past us, trying to save their own lives but offered me no assistance. After the planes had returned to their base of operation and people began to return to their homes, I found a local farmer who helped me to dig a shallow grave in which I buried my husband. Then I continued my flight westward.

"I had no idea where my two daughters and our only son were. But after months of careful inquiry I found that my son was in a temporary refugee college in the west and my daughters were attending another college. Snipers had shot at my son as he fled from home, but he fell on his face in the cornfields and crawled along on the ground until he was out of sight of the gunners. I was fortunate enough to find a place to teach science in a wartime medical college, but I was far away from my three children. Wages were low, and I had little money to send to help my children pay their expenses.

"Now, after four years, the long, destructive war is over and I have come back here to rebuild our home so that the children will eventually have a place to which they can come.

"After I reached here, I found that everything that remained after the bombings had been looted out of our store and even all of the bricks of the bombed buildings had been stolen and hauled away. Not a brick nor a piece of timber was left. With the little cash that I brought with me I have erected a tiny eight-by-ten-foot room. I called a builder to draw plans for a new store and a proper home for the family, and recently I discovered that he is trying to cheat me out of the little money I have left. Here I am a heartbroken widow, and everyone is trying to cheat me! What can I do? You still have your wife and family with you and have your medical practice on which you can depend as well as a dairy from which you can get support. But I have nothing. I am a lonesome widow who has lost everything, and they are trying to defraud me."

"Mrs. Goong," Dr. Chou replied, "'You need God — the true God. He can do for you what He did for me several years ago. I cannot answer all of the questions that are troubling you, but I have a friend here in the city who will. May I take you to her home and let her talk to you? She has helped my wife and me to know more about God. She is an American but she loves the Chinese people and is always glad to help them solve their problems. When can you go with me?"

"I can go at any time," she said. "What about tomorrow morning around nine o'clock?"

The next morning a refined, well-dressed Chinese woman appeared at our door with Dr. Chou. Over the tea cups she told me of her sorrows and worries. In response I told her of Christ who wanted to be her great burden bearer.

"But I don't believe in any god," she replied. "I am an atheist. Before I was married my parents worshiped idols, and after my marriage my husband's parents also worshiped the idols faithfully every day. But they always excused me from worship because they knew that I believed that idol worship was a waste of time and money."

Though we conversed together for three or more hours, she went off to her little house with the same unbelieving, troubled heart. Dr. Chou and I prayed together for her, that God would open her heart.

The following morning she and I had another apparently fruitless session together. But that evening I had a heavy burden on my heart for her salvation. Since I was to leave the next morning for another city and then go on my way for furlough in America, I felt I must see her saved before I left that city. Dr. Chou escorted me to her simple home. She invited us in. The furniture consisted of a folding canvas cot, a small table, a long wooden bench, a small trunk of clothing, and a small stand which held a wash basin. These articles of furniture filled her tiny room.

"Tomorrow I leave this city and will not return for some time," I told her. "I felt that we must have one more talk together before I leave."

Again we three talked back and forth. But each time she came back with her stock reply, "Don't forget that I am an atheist."

As the hour was getting late, I finally said, "Mrs. Goong, we want to pray with you before we leave. I will pray first, Dr. Chou will pray second, and then you please pray."

"How can I pray when I don't believe that there is a God?" she asked.

"Kneel down and pray anyway," I said. "As you

pray, God will reveal himself to you and let you know that there is a true God."

After Dr. Chou and I had prayed, I said to Mrs. Goong who was kneeling beside her cot, "Now you pray, Mrs. Goong. God will reveal himself to you as you pray."

She bowed her head and closed her eyes. "O God," she said. Then she lifted her head, looked at us and embarrassedly laughed aloud. "How can I pray to a God in whom I don't believe?" she asked. "I feel so foolish."

"Be honest with God and tell Him that you are an atheist and ask Him to reveal himself to you," I replied. "Forget that Dr. Chou and I are here and talk directly to God. He will lift your burden."

Again she bowed her head in prayer. "O God," she said, "You know that I don't believe in any god either Chinese or Western. But I need a refuge. If you are genuine, please reveal yourself to me."

With a radiant face she clasped her hands in joy and, turning to Dr. Chou and me, said, "God is real! Oh, He is real! I feel Him in my heart. I must talk to Him some more." With bowed head she told Him about her sorrows and heartaches and then asked us, "What is the polite, reverent way to close off the prayer?"

"Just say, 'In Jesus' name, Amen,' " I replied. She repeated it.

A radiant woman arose from her knees. Jesus had come to her heart. Dr. Chou and I soon took our leave after showing her where to read in the Bible that we gave her.

Early the next morning she was at our house. She called, "I had to come and tell you how I spent the night. I was so happy that I could hardly sleep. I have never experienced anything like this. God is genuine, and I now know Him personally. I am no longer an atheist."

She and the friends who had come early to escort us to the railroad station rejoiced together. We stood informally in a circle and prayed together before we got into the waiting rickshas and went off to the station. She joined the others who escorted us to the railroad station.

Shortly before the train left, she placed a letter addressed to her son in my hand, saying, "Please take this letter with you and mail it when you get off the train at your destination. My son is there attending college. I have asked him to come to the home where you will be staying so that you can help him to find this genuine joy that I am experiencing."

The day after our arrival at the next city, two fine college students appeared at our door. They were carrying the letter that we had mailed to Mrs. Goong's son.

"Are you Mrs. Taylor?" one asked. "My mother wrote and asked me to come and see you. She said that you have brought her great joy by introducing her to Jesus. Her life has been sad for several years since our family became disrupted and scattered. But she writes that she is happy since she found Jesus."

The two young men — Mrs. Goong's son and his cousin — and I talked over several Bible passages, and that afternoon both of them prayed and found peace with God. Each day afterward while we remained in that city, they continued to bring their classmates to our house where we helped them to repent and find God.

Mrs. Goong wrote letters to her two daughters who were still attending colleges in west China, advising them to find a Christian group near their campuses. It was not long until both of them were saved and became active in winning others to Christ.

Mrs. Goong became an avid student of the Bible.

For several years she did much house-to-house evangelism in which she brought many of her neighbors and acquaintances to the Lord. She became more active in telling her neighbors and friends about the living God who can save from all sin than she had ever been in advocating atheism. Her natural refinement coupled with her radiant joy in Christ made her a welcome visitor in many homes. The converted atheist was able to lead many into a vital relationship with the living God.